· THE ILLUSTRATED ·
DANCE TECHNIQUE OF
JOSÉ LIMÓN

· THE ILLUSTRATED ·
DANCE TECHNIQUE OF
JOSÉ LIMÓN

BY DANIEL LEWIS

DESCRIPTIVE TEXT WRITTEN
IN COLLABORATION WITH LESLEY FARLOW

LABANOTATION BY MARY COREY

DRAWINGS BY EDWARD C. SCATTERGOOD

HARPER & ROW, PUBLISHERS, NEW YORK
CAMBRIDGE, PHILADELPHIA, SAN FRANCISCO, LONDON, MEXICO CITY, SÃO PAULO, SYDNEY

Grateful acknowledgment is made for permission to reprint:

Excerpts from "Dance" by Deborah Jowitt first appeared in
The Village Voice, November 18, 1971. Copyright © 1971 by *The
Village Voice*; excerpts from "Allies of the Ground; Eye on the
Sky" by Deborah Jowitt first appeared in *The Village Voice*,
November 15, 1973. Copyright © 1973 by *The Village Voice*.
Reprinted by permission of the author and *The Village Voice*.

Excerpts from "Composing a Dance" by José Limón first
appeared in *The Juilliard Review*, Volume II, Number 1, Winter
1955. Reprinted by permission of the Juilliard School.

Photo page 2: José Limón in his last performance of Othello in The
Moor's Pavane *(1969).*

Photo page 6: José Limón in The Traitor.

Photo Credits:

Daniel Lewis: pages 2, 10–11, 12, 32–33, 34, 152–153, 168,
    170, 179, 184
Edward Effron: pages 6, 166, 167, 175, 176
Peter Schaaf: pages 68, 80, 115, 151
Milton Oleaga: pages 162, 177
Jane Rady: page 169
Radford Bascombe: pages 56–57, 136
Martha Swope: pages 158–159, 163
Birgit: page 161
Gjon Mili: page 165

THE ILLUSTRATED DANCE TECHNIQUE OF JOSÉ LIMÓN. Copyright ©
1984 by Daniel Lewis. Labanotation copyright © 1984 by the
Dance Notation Bureau. All rights reserved. Printed in the United
States of America. No part of this book may be used or
reproduced in any manner whatsoever without written
permission except in the case of brief quotations embodied in
critical articles and reviews. For information address Harper &
Row, Publishers, Inc., 10 East 53rd Street, New York, N.Y.
10022. Published simultaneously in Canada by Fitzhenry &
Whiteside Limited, Toronto.

FIRST EDITION

Design by Joel Avirom

Library of Congress Cataloging in Publication Data

Lewis, Daniel.
    The illustrated dance technique of José Limón.

    Bibliography: p.
    1. Ballet dancing.   2. Limón, José.   3. Choreography.
I. Farlow, Lesley.   II. Title.
GV1788.L46   1984   792.8'2'0924 [B]   83-48365
ISBN 0-06-015185-4   84 85 86 87 88 10 9 8 7 6 5 4 3 2 1
ISBN 0-06-091154-9 (pbk.) 84 85 86 87 88 10 9 8 7 6 5 4 3 2 1

*This book is dedicated
to my parents,
Jerome and Louise Lewis,
and is for
my artistic parents,
José Limón and Martha Hill*

Contents

Acknowledgments

For their help in bringing this book to pass, I would like to express my debt to my wife, Jane Carrington, for her knowledgeable comments on the technique, for modeling for the illustrations and for her support and tolerance throughout this project; to Lesley Farlow, for helping me put my thoughts into words and for other invaluable input; to Edward C. Scattergood for his exceptional ability to make a still drawing come alive; to Nancy Scattergood Jordan, my assistant and my right arm for the past eight years; to Mary Corey for her excellent notation of the exercises; to Reed Hansen, my accompanist of sixteen years, for his advice and for the notation of that musical accompaniment; to Sandra Dorr for her help in doing the historical research; and to June Dunbar, Laura Glenn and Lucy Venable.

I would like to thank the members of Daniel Lewis Dance: A Repertory Company for helping to carry on my approach to teaching, and my Juilliard students for being such able-bodied dancers and hard-working professionals.

I would also like to thank Charles Tomlinson for his help and encouragement, the Dance Collection of the New York Public Library for the Performing Arts for the use of their research facilities; the Limón family for their help and encouragement; Carla Maxwell of the José Limón Dance Foundation and all the countless dancers, choreographers and friends of the Limón tradition who, directly or indirectly, have contributed their time and energy to this project.

Most of all, I would like to thank Martha Hill for her guidance and encouragement and José Limón for sharing with me his work, which was his life.

Foreword

Walk into a studio where Daniel Lewis is teaching a class or directing a rehearsal—in New York, in London, in Los Angeles—and there's a quiet but insistent drive, a steady liveness that reflects commitment and clear direction. Positive. A fresh look. And a look that shows his inheritance from the great José Limón.

José Limón has been well recorded in photographs and reviews as a superb performer—one of the greatest of all time. He has an international reputation as the choreographer of a perfect dance work, *The Moor's Pavane*, which has been performed by top ballet and modern dance companies all over the world and is generally regarded as one of the great works of art in this century.

But José Limón, eloquent spokesman for dance, José Limón, teacher and innovator of a well-defined way of thinking about dance and dance style, Jose Limón, champion of the "discovery" of movement rather than the "invention" of movement—this José is too little known. Only those fortunate few who were close to him and to his daily work as an artist can pass Limón's "way" on to future generations. A gifted dancer and choreographer, Daniel Lewis is one of those fortunate few, and the one best equipped to record the technical approach to movement that José developed to build young dancers into instruments that could carry out not only his remarkable vision, but their own.

How can so complex an art and its craft and the teaching of that art be communicated? Daniel Lewis in his book has come at this problem through five avenues: related photographs that suggest style and atmosphere, drawings that strip down movement to its anatomic essentials and still incorporate beauty of motion, verbal description of sequence and detail, Labanotation to provide accurate and definite "notes" (as in a musical score) and, finally, notes to teachers, so important in humanizing the analytical nature of the task. I know of no study in our field which has "walked around" its subject and viewed it from so many frames of reference.

Here are lines of communication for "as many as will," as we say in English country dancing. We are grateful to Daniel Lewis for his dedication to an idea and for the years of experience which make this whole thing possible. José Limón would join him and me in saying, "Get it off the page and dance it."

Martha Hill
Director, Dance Division
The Juilliard School

Betty Jones and José Limón in the ending of The Moor's Pavane.

PART ONE

The Beginning

Dancers are part soldier, part gladiator, part matador. They possess the disciplined courage of the first, the brute daring of the second, the finesse of the last.

JOSÉ LIMÓN, "ON CONSTANCY"

José Limón rehearsing
The Winged *at the*
Washington Cathedral.

The Art of José Limón: A Brief History

Of the man as a dancer, what will be recalled? When I first saw him dance he was 48 years old, and still, I imagine, pretty much at his best. His dancing had a quality that can best be expressed as moral fervor. He had a magnificently sculptured head, and a body that seemed to brood. So far as his presence went, it could, perhaps, in our day and age, be compared on dance terms only with the ballet dancer Léonide Massine. It was hypnotic, even more, it was almost tangible.

CLIVE BARNES, "AS A DANCER, AN EAGLE"

When the prestigious Capezio Dance Award was presented to José Limón in 1964, the selection committee cited him as "a great dancer-choreographer whose years of intense struggle for recognition have culminated in his position as indisputably the foremost male dancer of his generation (the third) in the field of American modern dance."

The Award also honors not only the first dancer but the first artist to perform abroad—just ten years ago—under the auspices of the Cultural Presentations Program of the U.S. Department of State. . . . In paying tribute to Mr. Limón, the Capezio Dance Award recognizes a man who has . . . fought for the art of dancing as a creative force . . . who has introduced the great values of his Latin American heritage into the contemporary American dance theatre and who, as a descendant of the earliest Americans, has linked, through his dance art, our ancient past with our adventuresome present.[1]

During his lifetime José Limón, who received a *Dance Magazine* award for his choreographic contributions and three honorary doctorates from American universities, choreographed seventy-four works. Twenty—including such famous pieces as *The Moor's Pavane, Missa Brevis, The Unsung* and *The Exiles*—still exist in the contemporary repertories of the Limón Company, Daniel Lewis Dance, and such ballet companies as the Swedish Ballet, the Royal Danish Ballet, the American Ballet Theatre, the Joffrey

Ballet, the Pennsylvania Ballet and Les Grands Ballets Canadiens.

But José Limón left more to the dance world than a collection of marvelous dances and the memory of his own powerful performances. He developed a technique, a specific style of dancing, that could be passed on to future generations of dancers and choreographers.

Throughout his career, José touched hundreds of audiences with dances that expressed a profound understanding and respect for the joy and pain of human experience. In his own words, he sought "demons, saints, martyrs, apostates, fools and other impassioned visions"[2] to shape his choreography. To him, dance was more than a series of well-executed and ingeniously shaped movements; it was the inevitable expression of the human spirit. As Louis Chapin wrote, "He shakes like trees the big, rebellious questions in his life, and finds choreography his best hope of answering them."[3] Limón's dancers were taught to transcend their rigorous technical training in order to find their own dramatic and emotional motivations for dance. Men in particular responded to José's dancing because they saw in it a freedom, a male passion and strength, that ventured beyond the partnering role found in ballet and had a depth that was conspicuously absent from most Broadway show dancing. Limón's choreography sought a complete range of expression for both the male and the female body—from strength and sheer physicality to tenderness and gentleness.

When José Limón first arrived in New York in 1928, he had no intention of becoming a dancer or a choreographer. He had left home and family and university studies to pursue a career as a painter.

Born in 1908 in Culiacán, Sinaloa, Mexico, José Arcadio Limón was the oldest of eleven children. His father, Florencio Limón, was a musician of French and Spanish descent, and his mother, Francisca, came from a proper middle-class Mexican family with a bit of Yaquí Indian blood in its ancestry. The turmoil of the Mexican Revolution and the consequent closing of the Academia de Musica, where José's father worked, forced the family to emigrate in 1918. Their early years in the United States were arduous, and the Limóns spent some time traveling from place to place in the Southwest before finally settling down to a reasonably stable family life in Los Angeles.

José's musical gifts became evident early on. His father taught him to play the organ when José was still quite young, and he continued his studies in music throughout high school. But by the time he was ready to enter college, and with the encouragement of his art teacher, José had decided he wanted to be a painter. For a while he attended the University of California at Los Angeles as an art major, but ambition soon lured him to leave UCLA to pursue his career in New York.

With some friends from college—among them Perkins Harnly and

Don Forbes—the twenty-year-old aspiring painter arrived on the New York art scene at a time when Braque, Matisse and Dufy were all the rage and many American painters were heading for Europe to study. But El Greco and Michelangelo were José's idols. An incorrigible romantic, José simply didn't fit in, and what must have begun in a spirit of youthful adventure rapidly became a letdown. José made a living by working all manner of odd jobs, from modeling for fellow artists to running elevators. In between bouts with the paintbrushes, he fought off his growing frustrations by reading history and poetry, and by taking long daily runs—long before jogging was fashionable—up and down Riverside Drive.

Though European visual and performing artists were garnering the majority of the public's attention and support in 1928, three Americans were beginning to make history in the field of dance. Two of them, Doris Humphrey and Charles Weidman, had just left the Denishawn Company, along with pianist and costume designer Pauline Lawrence. The third was Martha Graham, who had left Denishawn five years earlier and was by then giving her own studio concerts.

The Denishawn Company, formed by Ruth St. Denis and her partner and husband, Ted Shawn, was known for its ethnically derivative pageants, replete with authentic costumes, elaborate lighting and stage sets. The dancing drew its movements from ethnic and folk dances from around the world—the Near East, the Orient, Spain, Africa and elsewhere. St. Denis, who once said that she wanted to "dance God," created choreography that tended to have a mystical, religious quality to it (in fact, her legal name was Ruth Dennis; her professional name came about when an early colleague dubbed her "Saint" Denis). Together, Ruth St. Denis and Ted Shawn established the Denishawn School, in which dancers were trained in styles that ranged from ballet to ethnic and "primitive" to St. Denis's own eclectic style. Through the school and through extensive touring all over the United States, Europe and the Orient, Denishawn provided a widely recognized alternative to ballet as serious concert dance. Though the work was eclectic and relatively derivative—in its exoticism it reflected aspects of art nouveau—Denishawn was serious, professional and innovative, and it is widely acknowledged as the first "modern" dance company.

Martha Graham, Doris Humphrey and Charles Weidman each felt that there could be yet other alternatives to ballet, however. They believed dance could and should express themes more directly connected to their lives, to their own heritage as Americans. They left Denishawn to pursue their individual ideals, to develop new subjects for choreography and, eventually, new vocabularies of movement.

Of this great second generation in modern dance, Martha Graham's name is the most familiar today. Though her earliest work showed the influence of Denishawn, as she experimented and gained real artistic independence she focused upon the structure and function of the body—on the physiological effects of breathing and on the function of contraction and release in the muscles, especially those in the back and abdomen. A vigorous physicality came to be the trademark of her distinctive vocabulary of movement. As Don McDonagh has written, "In the public's mind dancers were light, ethereal creatures. Graham, however, deployed a squad of strong, powerful women who pounded the earth, rebounded from it, and strode rather than glided across it. She created dances that launched these women like battering rams against the stage conventions of the day. Glamour was definitely out."[4]

Extraordinarily angular and percussive, this austere style was Graham's declaration of independence from Denishawn's Oriental exoticism and a clear repudiation of the decorative aspect of ballet. Though her work would indeed expand to include solos, male dancers and softer and more lyric expressions, at this stage Graham's "signature" was a concentration upon movement by a group of dancers—all women—performing as a unit, with Graham as the central figure. "The look of the Group was that of gaunt, iron-willed Puritans. And as the Puritans had hewn living space out of a wilderness, so Graham and her Group would clear artistic space for succeeding generations."[5]

Five years after Graham's departure from the Denishawn Company, Doris Humphrey, Charles Weidman and Pauline Lawrence—inhibited in their attempts to pursue their own artistic ideas within the Denishawn organization—left to form the Humphrey-Weidman studio. In theoretical terms, Doris spoke of dance as the movement of the body through space, from standing to lying, as it responded to the pull of gravity. In resistance to gravity lay the seeds of dance. The thrill and drama came from the defiance of gravity, the moment of suspension when the body seemed to break free of its physical confines. Doris called this spectrum of movement "the arc between two deaths."

By studying the ebb and flow of the breath and how it affects movement, she developed a sense of the body's natural rhythms and explored how fall and recovery occur as a manifestation of those rhythms. From these principles she built a style of movement that was flowing, rhythmic and dramatic. Charles's wit and brilliant improvisational and mimetic talent added realistic, everyday gesture and humor to Doris's more formal concerns and lyrical style. Together the group explored rhythm, accompaniment, gesture and the possibilities for dramatic communication.

As a choreographer Doris chose themes that ranged from the formal and the abstract, as in *Color Harmony*, to explorations of human experience, as in *The Shakers*. She was concerned with the meaning of experience as it was manifested in action and movement, in dancing "from the inside out," and she encouraged her students to express their own imaginations and experiences in their dancing. At the same time Doris's extraordinary sense of design, of the range of possibility in formal constructions by a group of dancers, gave form to her ideas.

Water Study, choreographed in 1928, illustrates how she used natural breath rhythms. She wrote in the program notes: "Probably the thing that distinguishes musical rhythm from other rhythm is the measured time beat, so this has been eliminated from the Water Study and the rhythm flows in natural phrases instead of cerebral measures. There is no count to hold the dancers together in the very slow opening rhythm, only the feel of the wavelength that curves the backs of the groups."[6]

The dancers began grouped in a kneeling position, allowing the rhythm of their collective breathing to gently lift their backs, and gradually to raise their bodies higher and higher as the momentum built, until the power of the breath tossed the dancers' bodies across the stage.

Dances by these early companies were infrequently performed in theaters because of the expense of renting one and the difficulty of obtaining a forum for the still-experimental art of modern, or "interpretive," dance, which could offer little box office competition for ballet or for European performers. More often than not, performances took place in the studios where classes were taught and rehearsals held. When formal concerts were given, they had to be offered on Sundays, when the theaters were available and cheap to rent. And because of New York's blue laws which forbade Sunday entertainments, they were billed as "sacred concerts." Ruth St. Denis's urge to "dance God" may have provided a useful historic precedent in dealing with this problem. Don McDonagh, in his book on Martha Graham, described the situation:

> The new generation of dancers was creating an art form out of its native experience, and it was doing so without any public support. Idealistic, it was headed for the poorhouse. . . .
>
> For modern dancers . . . ballet was frivolous and, harshest of words, European. It was not relevant to the twentieth century. Modern was serious, relevant, and American.
>
> Unfortunately, the public of the time did not much like American, and it cared equally little for modern. Any foreign artist or art was considered superior to any American artist or art. . . . As a result, many American painters, instrumentalists, and singers went to Europe in order to further their careers back home. But this option simply was not open to modern dancers; the art in which they were working did not exist in Europe. Denishawn had been able to go to Europe to collect favorable notices before embarking on an American tour, but it was working within a format familiar to European audiences, which had been extensively exposed to exotic dancers from the Middle and Far East. . . . Poor from the start, modern dance learned to live without money.[7]

But there was some experimentation in dance going on in Europe, particularly in Germany, and the German Expressionist dancer Harald Kreutzberg was one of the Europeans who got some attention in America. When he came to New York in 1928, he appeared at the New Yorker Theatre.

Kreutzberg was a student of Mary Wigman, a German modern dancer whose work dealt with symbolic and psychological themes. His dancing combined the strength of a rigorous balletic training with an extraordinary ability to convey emotion by the simplest of movements. For one young painter, whose friends had coerced him into attending the concert, the German dancer's performance was electrifying. José had never seen anyone, and certainly never a grown man, move like this. With all the impulsiveness and romanticism of his nature, José Limón decided then and there to become a dancer.

José's friends, well aware of his frustrations with painting, encouraged this new-found ambition. Perkins Harnley knew Charles Weidman from high school days in Nebraska—a real bit of luck for José, since at the time the Humphrey-Weidman Studio was one of the few that accepted male students.

When José first walked into the studio on Tenth Street, he was introduced to Pauline Lawrence, the studio's accompanist, who would eventually become his wife, costume designer, adviser and, as he put it, his "best friend and most uncompromising critic." And in Doris Humphrey and Charles Weidman he met two people who would quickly change his life.

As one of only a small number of male dancers, José soon found himself in the heady but no doubt frightening position of having to perform before he'd had much training. Twenty is an advanced age at which to begin serious dance training, but blessed with a natural athletic ability, José dove into the work with an intensity that may have occasionally alarmed his classmates. At six feet and some-odd inches tall with a powerful build, he had to learn to control his body and his weight within the Humphrey-Weidman technique. John Martin—the first dance critic at the *New York Times* and an early and important champion of modern dance—described José as a "tyro" in his dancing class, "not unlike one of his native Mexican bulls in a china shop."

He was physically tense, far too energetic, could not take a relaxed movement if he tried, and worked much too hard at everything. But apparently his innate gifts were visible to the experienced eye, for within a month, though he knew virtually nothing, he was in the back lines of "Lysistrata" in the dances Miss Humphrey had directed for the famous Norman Bel Geddes production. There he remained for the entire nine months of the run.[8]

Of his classes with Doris, José wrote:

> With her low, yet commanding voice and coolly serene manner, she would teach us both theory and practice. With tremendous lucidity she would explain the principles on which she was basing her technical exercises. Fall and recovery. Breath. Suspension. Tension and relaxation. Breath phrase. Breath rhythm. Always the breath. She moved like a gazelle.
>
> It was fortunate for me that Miss Humphrey's partner, Charles Weidman, was a totally different artist. She was in essence a formalist. He was an expressionist. In his classes all technical exercises were devoted toward a species of extended pantomime which had a puckish or comic flavor. I remember that there was a great deal of fun and laughter. He was a superb mimic and clown. His objectives and methods I found painfully difficult, contrary to my over-serious natural inclinations, and I found myself always inept and stupid.

José went on to describe Charles:

> [He was] always interested in the intrinsic capacities of the male dancer, and devoted much thought and time to devising a syllabus of technical studies quite distinct from that of the women. . . . At the studio there was much concern with the weight and substance of the body. Both our teachers abandoned the traditional concept that a dancer should appear to be free of all gravitational pull, his movement devoid of all seeming effort. The weight of the body should be recognized and exploited. . . . Elevation, soaring into the air, would in consequence have more drama, more meaning. It would become a triumph, a conquest.[9]

In solving his early problems with technique, José began to conceive of the human body in motion as an orchestra, the different parts of the body as the many instruments. This became a central concept in his approach to dancing and teaching. The process of learning how to move and how to dance became the process of learning how to play each of these instruments, first separately and then in harmony, in order to create the full orchestra. He developed a series of exercises that isolated the different parts of the body, so that he could learn how to control the weight within each body part as he moved. This consciousness of weight, and the sense of power behind it, was remarked upon by critics throughout José's career and became a trademark of his style. The system as he later taught it dealt with the complex distribution of weight in the body and added a new dimension to the development of Doris's and Charles's original techniques.

The company was an interesting and complicated gathering of talents. José was ardent about tragedy, Charles was ardent about comedy, and Doris was as determined as Gertrude Stein to establish emotional and intellectual expression in her own style. At the studio neither Doris nor Charles was as interested in developing a "technique" as they were in exploring the human body's potential for movement and in developing that potential to express new choreographic ideas. Nevertheless these experiments eventually led to the development of a very specific approach to movement, combining Doris's concern with analyzing the relationship of the body to gravity and the way the body moves through space with Charles's use of dynamics, weight and gesture. The result is what is referred to as the Humphrey-Weidman technique. But Doris's and Charles's different approaches to movement initially constituted two separate techniques, used interchangeably when they choreographed for the company. Part of the Humphrey-Weidman philosophy was that a work is never finished, that it constantly develops and grows in performance. They felt the same was true of technique—that the movement taught in class was part of a constant process of discovery and development—and they encouraged their dancers to explore their own approaches to the style.

Two years after he started taking classes, José presented his first two choreographic works: *Étude in D Flat Major,* a duet composed to Alexander Scriabin's music of the same name and performed by José and Letitia Ide, and *Bacchanale,* set to an original percussion score by José and performed by Ernestine Henoch (later Stodelle), Eleanor King and Letitia Ide.

These early student works—solos, duets and trios—primarily dealt with pure movement. That is, José was experimenting with what his body was beginning to accomplish as a dancer. His painter's eye composed the groupings of dancers; the musical structures came easily from his early training and lifelong love of music.

Passionate, talented and impetuous, José found the perfect mentor in Doris Humphrey, whose cool hand restrained and guided him while at the same time she gave him all the encouragement he needed. Under her tutelage, José quickly "built a reputation for a commanding stage presence, a gift for moving like a finely tuned animal, and for dignity and sincerity."[10] He soon became a full-fledged member of the Humphrey-Weidman Company, appearing in such works as *New Dance, Theatre Piece* and *Passacaglia,* touring and teaching.

In the summers the company went to Bennington, Vermont, where the six-week Bennington School and Dance Festival were held. The Bennington Festival was the first, and for years the only, event of its kind. It was the brilliant idea of two educators: Martha Hill, a former member of Martha Graham's company who taught in the dance program at NYU, and Robert Devore Leigh, the first president of Bennington College. The Bennington College trustees approved the establishment of a "modern dance center." Coordinated by Martha Hill, Director, Mary Josephine Shelly, Administrative Director, and Martha Biehle, chief fundraiser for Bennington who became the Executive Secretary, the first school was scheduled for the summer of 1934. Classes in the different modern dance styles were to be taught, as well as classes in dance history, music and dance, and composition and choreography. Faculty for the center would be chosen from the prime innovators in modern dance, criticism and music for dance.

It's hard to overestimate the value of this development in the modern dance world. The festival offered the choreographers, who had little or no work during the summer season, the chance to create new works on their companies, whose room and board was paid and who were there expressly for the purpose of dancing. There would be no need to juggle rehearsal schedules with the dancers' full-time work schedules, no recruiting students, no rushing around on subways and buses searching for theaters and rehearsal spaces, no worry about finding the money to rent them.

The first Bennington School of the Dance opened its doors with a stellar faculty that included Martha Graham, Hanya Holm, Doris Humphrey and Charles Weidman, who would each teach dance for two weeks of the session. Louis Horst was there to teach music, and John Martin offered classes in dance history. At this early stage there was a certain rivalry between the dance teachers, each of whom felt his or her style was the only way to dance. It's a safe bet that many of those first Bennington students, most of whom were dance teachers attached to physical education departments, left the festival in an initial state of confusion. Despite that, the festival proved an artistic and financial success.

In succeeding years, as the Bennington School of the Dance grew and aspiring dancers began to take over the student population at the festival, Bennington became the training ground for members of some of the modern dance companies. As it gained in popularity and artistic stature, the festival was able to offer choreographic fellowships to artists of the next generation whose work was judged of promisingly high quality. José Limón, Anna Sokolow and Esther Junger received the first Bennington fellowships, awarded in 1937.

Then, in 1940, after more than a decade of growth and development with Humphrey-Weidman, a deep personal rift with Charles spurred José to break with the company and leave New York to strike out on his own. He returned to California, where he moved in with old college friends and for a time teamed up with former Graham dancer and choreographer May O'Donnell. Together they created several works which they toured up and down the West Coast. May's husband, composer Ray Green, created the scores for these new works. It was a happy collaboration of two choreographers and one composer.

Meantime an intense correspondence was developing between Pauline Lawrence and José, and after a year she joined José in San Francisco. There they were married on October 13, 1941, and a new phase of José's career began. From that point on Pauline dedicated herself and her formidable talents to furthering José's career with dreams of eventually forming a company and a school. Her first goal was to convince José to return to the East, where he was known and respected as a dancer. Evidently she had little trouble winning him over to the plan, and by the next fall she had located an apartment for them in New York.

Doris welcomed José back to the company, which was still called the Humphrey-Weidman Company, although by this time Doris and Charles had begun to go their separate ways. José took his place as the lead dancer, dancing both old and new roles, and in 1942 he created the solo work *Chaconne*. The dance was inspired by the work of José's favorite composer, "the supremely choreographic composer, that incomparable dancer of the spirit, J. S. Bach."[11] The music was Bach's "Chaconne" from the *Partita #2 in D Minor for Unaccompanied Violin. Dance Observer* reviewed the December 1942 performance at Studio Theatre:

> What seemed at first a dazzling and presumptuous dance stunt, José Limón's *Chaconne* turned out to be an extraordinary and successful venture in dilating the region of the modern dance. Actually, the work is a duet, the first (I think) of its kind, in which Roman Totenberg, violinist, and José Limón, dancer, count equally and in visual and dramatic conjunction. As the lights go on, there is the violinist downstage left and the dancer upstage right. Between them is the diagonal line, asserted from the beginning, giving the point and key to the whole dance, and there at the end, triumphantly affirmed.[12]

This was the first work in which José found a way to set his inventive movements in a strong emotional and thematic context. One of his finest pieces, *Chaconne* marked the beginning of his maturing as a choreographer.

But the United States was at war, and José, a naturalized American citizen, was soon drafted. He ended up at Fort Lee, Virginia, in the Special Services, where he worked with combat troops and continued to choreograph, doing camp shows for servicemen. One show, *Song of the Medics*, included a classic number called "This is a Machete, Eddie." On every leave that José had, he headed to New York to continue with his serious choreography.

By the time José was discharged from the Army, Doris had stopped dancing completely because of severe arthritis and had turned both the studio and the school over to Charles Weidman. José, whose rift with Charles had never quite healed, was ready in any event to strike out on his own, and Pauline was there to encourage him to form his own company. He invited soloist and choreographer Pauline Koner to work with him, along with Letitia Ide, Beatrice Seckler, Miriam Pandor, Lucas Hoving and, later, Betty Jones and Ruth Currier. Doris Humphrey herself now turned to José and his new company as the answer to the continuation of her dance career, and she began to choreograph for the newly formed Limón Company.

The *Lament for Ignacio Sánchez Mejías* was the first of many powerful works that Doris created for the company. A dramatic piece based on the Federico García Lorca poem about the death of a bullfighter, it was first performed in 1946. *The Story of Mankind,* a duet for José and Beatrice Seckler, followed later that year. *Day on Earth* premiered in 1947, danced by José, Letitia Ide and Miriam Pandor, with Melissa Nicolaides as The Child.

The first piece that José Limón choreographed and performed with his new company was *La Malinche,* based on a Mexican legend of love, politics and betrayal, and danced by José, Lucas Hoving and Pauline Koner. In *La Malinche* José went to his own Mexican heritage for the story; the themes of revolution, political intrigue and betrayal would resurface in his later work. The dance was not a literal rendering of the plot: José's interest lay in the essence of each character, and the dance movement was an exploration of the dramatic motivation and interplay among the characters in the story.

Four members of the early company—Lucas Hoving, Pauline Koner, Betty Jones and Ruth Currier—were to stay with José for periods of up to twenty years. Each had a particular quality as a dancer: Pauline, a strong, independent and creative soloist; Betty, a beautiful, technically brilliant dancer; Ruth, powerfully lyrical; and Lucas, whose humor and light strength became a perfect foil for José on stage. All worked together to form a strong, versatile company. José's ability to recognize and use a dancer's own special strengths and qualities made working for him both challenging and satisfying, and his dancers responded by performing beautifully and remaining loyal to him for years. Betty would continue to make guest appearances through 1969, and Ruth would return a year after José's death in 1972 to take over artistic direction of the company. Five years later Lucas would come back as artistic adviser.

Between 1946 and her death in 1958, Doris Humphrey served as artistic director and created some of her greatest works for the Limón Company: *Night Spell, Ritmo Jondo, Ruins and Visions.* Under Doris's careful and expert guidance, José's works premiered at the American Dance Festival at Connecticut College in New London, which opened in 1948. This was actually a revival of the Bennington Festival, which had closed down during the war. The reputation of the festival was now firmly established, and each summer dancers and choreographers came from all over the country to participate. New York dance critics made the trip from the city at the end of each session to review the new works.

There, in 1949, José choreographed and premiered his masterpiece and signature work, *The Moor's Pavane.* Based on the story of Othello and structured as a court dance, a pavane, the piece brought into brilliant focus Limón's skill at exploring a dramatic situation through the medium of pure dance. The progression of the plot is clear, but it is the movement itself, and the spatial paths and patterns of the dancers that indicate the covert alliances and complex emotions that motivate each character. More than twenty years after its first performance, Clive Barnes in the *New York Times* praised the piece as a "dance of truly Shakespearean dimension."

> There is a lovely quality here of passion and fever. Few ballets have quite this concentrated pungency, this passionate elegance. The complete theme of "Othello," love, jealousy, betrayal and death, is captured within the measures of a stately pavane.[13]

Set to the music of Henry Purcell, the *Pavane* was hailed by critics for its "disciplined and economic movement" and "details of dramatic pacing and facial characterization."

> The action is close-knit, intense, without a wasted gesture or an unnecessary development, yet there is a great variety of mood and movement and a steady building to the inevitable climax. The individual characters have the utmost clarity and their movement is extraordinarily evocative under the dark, rather smothering atmosphere which envelops it.[14]

The *Pavane* made brilliant use of the specific skills of Limón's company: Betty Jones as the delicate, innocent Desdemona; Pauline Koner as the troubled Emilia. Lucas Hoving performed an elegant, treacherous Iago, and José danced a powerful Moor, "drawing himself up from a wide-legged plié into balance on one straight leg, as if the ground held him back, or as if the air were too thick to move through," as *Village Voice* critic Deborah Jowitt later observed. "That kind of awareness of the pull of gravity made him—and his dances—look powerful: the struggle of muscles became a metaphor for the struggle of souls."[15]

As a dancer José was reaching his peak, and in April 1949 *New York Times* critic John Martin wrote that José Limón was "at the top of his class."

> There is no other male dancer within even comparing distance of him. He is magnificent looking, and utterly un-Hollywood. His face is rugged, modeled, sensitively responsive, mature. He is handsomely built, and moves with the easy command of a fine animal; his gesture is simple and broad, his dynamics and phrasing are beautifully controlled, his responses are extremely musical, there is a complete honesty of feeling behind his movement, as well as an emotional intensity that projects itself eloquently. He conquers a demanding repertoire with a vital and persuasive mastery.[16]

It was a fruitful and hectic period for the whole company. José, Betty Jones and Ruth Currier had begun teaching classes in New York at the Dance Players Studios. As the tour schedule intensified, Lucy Venable and June Dunbar took over classes and kept the studio going while the company was on the road. José also gave master classes on the road and, along with company members, taught flocks of young dancers who arrived each summer to study at Connecticut College. For José, classes were a time in which to experiment and develop new movement. His technique reflected his choreographic ideas; the imagery he used was dramatic rather than physical. "Reach further," he would say, rather than "Lift higher." He urged his students to try to extend their physical limits, and by doing so to use their own abilities to further develop the movement he taught. Students were encouraged to find the meaning of the dance movement for themselves, infusing each arch of the back, lift of the arm or drop of the upper body with a dramatic, even spiritual, quality that came from within.

By now José had become something of a public figure. There was a brooding, aristocratic elegance about him in the published photos of the period, and certainly in the public eye he cut a darkly romantic figure. But in his personal and professional relationships he was expansive and generous, loved giving gifts, loved trading corny jokes—backstage, between classes or sitting up front in the tour bus sharing a thermos of martinis with his close friend Simon Sadoff, the company's musical director. In a 1953 *New York Times* Sunday Magazine article John Martin asked, "What is a great male dancer like personally?"

> Limón for the most part is not the conventional type, whatever that may be. He is large, healthy, comfortably and casually dressed, without a hint of personal vanity. He laughs easily, is witty and hearty, and he eats with that unromantic appetite common to dancers. Just as in his dancing an innate gentleness and discipline hold in check his dynamic forcefulness, so in his personal manner an unusual courteousness contains his natural strength.[17]

The next major development for the Limón Company was a residency in Mexico City sponsored by the Instituto Nacional de Bellas Artes. The artist Miguel Covarrubias, whom José had met years earlier in New York City, had since returned to Mexico and assumed the directorship of the Institute. In 1951 he invited the Limón Company to perform and choreograph at the Palacio de Bellas Artes, with the support of the Mexican Government. This honor presented José with his first opportunity to experiment with large ensemble works, most of which were based on Mexican themes, and with the dynamic rhythms of Mexico's music. He used both the members of his own company and Mexican dancers for the thirty-person cast of *Los Cuatros Soles* and the twenty-six person cast of *Redes*.

Despite its successes, the Limón Company, like most dance companies, had to deal with constantly fluctuating financial circumstances. So in 1951, when Martha Hill, head of the Juilliard dance department, asked José to join the faculty of the Juilliard School of Music to teach and choreograph, it was a golden opportunity for him to continue his creative work without the struggle of maintaining an independent studio. Pauline reluctantly gave up the idea of an independent Limón school of dance, and José accepted the position.

This was a time of great productivity for Limón. With Doris acting as his adviser, editor and choreographic guide, he choreographed works both for his Juilliard students and for the Limón Company and kept up a schedule of performance and teaching tours that took him all over the United States. Every summer at Connecticut College he created a new work for the Dance Festival, where *The Exiles*, *The Visitation*, *The Traitor*, *Scherzo* and *Blue Roses*, among others, premiered. During this period a number of men joined the company—Michael Hollander, Harlan McCallum and Chester Wolenski among them—and José choreographed pieces such as *The Traitor* and *Scherzo* specifically for a male cast.

Then in 1954 the State Department invited the Limón Company to participate in the department's cultural exchange program by touring South America. Here was genuine tangible recognition on the part of the "establishment," and it was an early watershed, not just for the Limón Company but for modern dance in general. Fruitful as the fifties were, modern dance was still a relatively emergent art, and very few major companies were holding their own. Then, as now, most dancers—especially those with no academic ties—had to seek "regular" work outside of dance to pay the rent, and most modern choreographers had to turn to Broadway and popular choreography for their bread and butter.

A second invitation, this time to tour Europe, came in 1957. In between these tours a commission from the Empire State Music Festival led to the creation of *The Emperor Jones*, based on the O'Neill play and destined to become one of the Limón Company's perennial crowd pleasers. José worked with composer Heitor Villa-Lobos on an original score for this ballet in a collaboration that proved to be enormously successful. José then turned his attention to the choreography of *There Is a Time*, based on verses from Ecclesiastes, with music composed by Norman Dello Joio. *There Is a Time* toured European cities still devastated by World War II. There José became obsessed with the dreadful destruction in Eastern Europe, especially in Poland, where, he said, "four of her cities were still 85 percent uncleared rubble. I had no preparation for the shock of what I saw. I asked people in the streets, 'How can you stand being alive among this?' 'We have to,' they answered, 'We have to rebuild.'"[18]

The experience had an enormous impact on José, and he returned to the United States overwhelmed with complicated feelings of admiration, sorrow, anger and guilt. This was one of the "big questions" within his experience that could best be explored through his art, and out of it came *Missa Brevis*. Set to Zoltán Kodály's *Missa Brevis in Tempore Belli,* it marked the first time that José undertook a work entirely of his own—without soliciting Doris Humphrey's cherished advice.

In the piece the solo figure (danced by José) begins as a "tweed-jacketed bystander" who watches "a phalanx of dancers gradually responding to the rhythms of Kodály's richly appealing music, and to the words of the opening Kyrie. By the time the Gloria section has reached the words 'Qui tollis peccati mundi' (who bore the sins of the world), Mr. Limón is wholly involved, and bears the burden of interpretation as soloist, running, seeking, supplicating. . . . One's religious persuasion naturally affects his sense of the text itself. Yet Mr. Limón has translated it in terms not so much of liturgy as of questions and answers experienced by the aspiring human spirit."[19]

This was a period of high excitement and passionate creativity for José, who received the *Dance Magazine* Award in 1957, but it was brutally interrupted in 1958 with the death of Doris Humphrey. More than subdued by the loss of his great mentor, José found it difficult to create new work. His great energy found better focus in teaching at Juilliard, which became a training ground for new company members. By 1963, when another command performance took the company on a tour of Asia, José had added a group of younger dancers from Juilliard to his roster, and once the tour was completed, the composition of the company underwent a basic change: Pauline Koner had left in 1960 because of differences of opinion; now Betty Jones, Lucas Hoving and Ruth Currier left to pursue independent careers, shifting the emphasis to some of the newer dancers: Jennifer Muller, Louis Falco, Sarah Stackhouse and me. Though Betty would make guest appearances for years to come, the company was essentially a new Limón Company, composed of dancers already groomed in Limón technique from their years at Juilliard.

Other essential changes took place during the decade of the sixties. José, who saw in the fashionable counterculture something that mimicked the poverty of his childhood and the "mañana" attitude of the ghetto, railed at his younger company members about their "hippie" long hair and blue jeans. The aesthetics of dance were changing too, and the American press was giving a great deal of attention to the minimalists and their unemotional, formalist concerns, their rebellion against the use of trained dancers. At a time when Yvonne Rainer was making dances about sitting, walking and running to be performed by non-dancers, José, baffled by what he must have considered to be a non-aesthetic, continued to use trained bodies and very physical, demanding movement. The recognition and attention given the new generation of iconoclasts frankly upset and hurt him, but he stubbornly continued to explore the dramatic possibilities of dance and to adhere to his belief in the redemptive nature of art. Though the attention of the critics may have been focused elsewhere for a time, audiences all over the world continued to respond to José's work.

August 1964 marked José's visible emergence from this troubled time, when the American Dance Festival premiered *A Choreographic Offering*. Commissioned by the Festival, it was a tribute to Doris Humphrey, and it was the beginning of a real resurgence in José's creativity. This was the first piece José choreographed on the new company. Our pleasure in this, our reverence for José as an artist, the homage to Doris, the beauty of the piece—all combined to make the performance an extraordinarily moving experience for the dancers. The eight members of the company performed as soloists with a corps of twenty student dancers. During the finale, the soloists formed a processional moving diagonally across the stage, arms linked, heads and bodies bent over, performing the majestic movement motifs of Doris's dances. Each soloist would break away and return to the line, and each time the soloist passed through centerstage, he or she passed through a single spotlight, which represented Doris's presence. By the end of this passage, tears were streaming down all our faces.

It was in that same year that José Limón received the coveted Capezio Dance Award for his contributions to the art.

During the rocky period after Doris's death, a quiet, steady development in Limón technique had been taking place at Juilliard, with Betty Jones, Ruth Currier, Lucy Venable and June Dunbar adding some of their own ideas and helping José refine the technique. When José taught, he spent the first part of a class teaching the students how to isolate the different body parts and explore the limits of rotation, stretch and flexion. He then taught "across the floor" exercises in which students learned, while traveling across the floor, how to use all the parts of the body as a whole. This was an essential but difficult concept in the technique—what José called "the body as orchestra"—and many students had trouble with it. Betty Jones became the principal tutor in this area, teaching students how to move efficiently and properly, using the length of the muscles, and teaching the principles of alignment and breathing as developed by Lulu Sweigard, a pioneer in the field of movement analysis. In José's classes students concentrated on style and dynamics; in Betty's they learned how each part of the body relates to a central axis and how to use the central axis to balance and suspend. They discovered how to use the breath throughout the body to create a sensation of lightness as well as a sense of weight as they danced; how to use the breath rhythm in fall and recovery (as Doris taught it), but adding the isolation of different parts of the body (as José developed it).

As he worked with his students and his company, José began to gravitate toward more abstract themes in his choreography. Occasionally, if he got stuck, he would say to us, "Come here, children, and sit down." Thinking aloud for us, he'd explore or re-explore his ideas for the dance, the characters, where the piece was headed choreographically, what the problems were. During the making of *The Winged,* he would talk about Zeus, the gods, the Sphinx, Pegasus, as a way of articulating his thoughts and helping us to understand the dance.

An ensemble work for sixteen, choreographed in 1966, *The Winged* was about those mythical winged creatures, but its essential theme was, simply, flight. Not only was José beginning to experiment with more abstract themes and with works for larger ensembles, he was also experimenting with different concepts of music. Resistant as he was to the more radical minimalist movements of the sixties, he was not immune to the changes in the arts going on around him. Doris and José had always wanted to create a dance that could stand on its own without the need of musical accompaniment. This was his first work created for silence; he built it on breath phrasing and group rhythm. Later, afraid to go all the way without music, he created a sound collage for *The Winged:* electronic sounds, jazz, birds chirping, the sound of the wind. The collage served as "incidental music," a departure from his usual use of the rhythmic structure of the music to determine the basic choreographic structure of the dance.

By 1967 he was experimenting with spoken text, voice scores and taped speeches, and these were beginning to figure in his musical scores. The movement itself literally "poured out of him," and as the pace increased he began to use me as his assistant. After teaching me the movement as he had choreographed it, he'd coach me in instructional techniques and then I became responsible for the basic instruction of the rest of the company members. José took over again when actual rehearsals began. This division of labor was particularly useful when we were staging works on other companies and everyone's time was limited.

It was also necessary for José to conserve his strength. His creative outpouring during the late sixties was all the more fervent because he was now battling for time against cancer, the disease that would eventually claim both him and Pauline. In the fall of 1967 José entered the hospital for the first of several operations for cancer of the prostate, and although he continued to perform through 1968, by 1969 he had stopped dancing completely in order to devote himself solely to his choreography. As his cancer worsened, I took on many of his responsibilities, teaching classes at Juilliard and on the road, managing the company on tour, conducting rehearsals and, with Laura Glenn, Carla Maxwell and Jennifer Scanlon, staging José's work on different ballet and modern companies.

Of José's later works, *The Unsung* (1970) is a clear example of how he wove dramatic material into an abstract dance. As a tribute to the American Indian, *The Unsung* was created for a group of eight men to no accompaniment other than the sounds of the stamping, running, leaping, tapping and brushing of the dancers' feet and the sound of their breathing. An ensemble section was followed by a series of eight solos, each of which was named after a specific Indian hero: Metacomet, Pontiac, Tecumseh, Red Eagle, Black Hawk, Osceola, Sitting Bull and Geronimo. José had each dancer research the life of the character he was to create. As the dance developed, he had us imagine the hot desert sand burning our feet, the dry wind blowing across our faces, the immense distances of the desert. He spoke to us of the love and reverence the Indians have for the earth. We had to come to understand, in a deeply personal way, all we could of this heritage, this environment, so that, without a definite plot line, the piece would emerge in clear, physical manifestations of these feelings and images. Performed in silence, the movement became the music.

In many ways, *The Unsung* was a tribute to José's heritage as a Mexican and to his Yaquí Indian ancestry. The absence of music and the simplicity of structure made this a work of pure, rich dancing.

The Unsung may be spartan in its form, but each solo is rich and complicated. If the work is a roster of spirits, on another level it is a kind of glossary of Limón male-dancing. All the things you ever saw him do, plus all the things he ever wanted to do. The dancers project the pride, savagery, wariness of hunters who became the quarry, but there is little that is "primitive" in their movement. Except perhaps the reiterated rhythms of slaps and stamps and a few squared-off arm positions. Everything else is pure Limón: the spreading fingers, angled wrists, diving turns in attitude, the gestures that curl in quickly and expand on the slow release of a breath, above all the sense of weighty soaring. . . .

I didn't mean to imply that there is no contrast between solos. There is, and there is also a shrewd use of each dancer's particular quality. The assertive and impetuous dance performed by Peter Sparling is followed by a wonderfully hushed, low-swirling one by Louis Solino. And while Sparling is solid, but of a rubbery flexibility, Solino is delicate, precise, reserved in his carriage. And Solino is followed by Aaron Osborne in a solo that makes subtle use of his high extensions and long, curving line. Gary Masters' quick series of fluttering leaps (is he Black Hawk then?) precedes the solid, more earth-bound dancing of Edward de Soto, whose stamps punctuate the big-cat pulsing like grunts or growls. Daniel Lewis is springy, strong—driving his weight down into the floor and rebounding from the impact, but Ryland Jordan skims smoothly along the ground as if propelled by the twin circlings of his arms. . . .

The premiere performance of *The Unsung* was dedicated to Ted Shawn. As the great pioneer in choreography for men, he should be terribly pleased. It's not often these days that you see men dancing with this particular kind of beauty.[20]

During the next two years, the dances José created continued to mine the possibilities he had begun to explore in *The Unsung*. *Dances for Isadora* was another series of solos, each of which portrayed a different aspect of the legendary Isadora Duncan. Here, too, José acknowledged an artistic debt, to the woman he spoke of as his "artistic mother." *Orfeo,* choreographed in 1972, was a haunting work based on the story of Orpheus and Eurydice. The ending—an empty stage and an unfinished piece of music—was perhaps a statement of the grief he felt at the loss of his wife, Pauline, who had died in 1971.

His last work, *Carlota,* the story of Carlota and Maximilian and the Spanish conquest of Mexico, clearly returned to his earlier use of the dramatic story line. This time, though, it was danced in silence.

On December 2, 1972, while the company was performing in Honolulu, José Limón died in a hospital near his farm in Flemington, New Jersey.

Dancers who have worked with José Limón invariably say that he made each person feel special; he helped them discover and manifest their unique qualities. He was more concerned with the truth in his work and in the performance of it than the dancers' technical perfection, though his works were, and are, demanding of a dancer's strength. To this end, he taught a way of dancing that trained a dancer to use every part of his or her body as an expressive tool. His dancers learned always to probe for the dramatic and spiritual underpinnings of their movement. It was this quality that made his dancers look "slightly superhuman," in the sense of supremely human:

> . . . the men more masculine, the women more female, and all of them bigger than they are. It's not only because of the heroic themes he chooses. His movement style is expansive, employing unusual power in the men's arms and upper torsos. The dancers often seem to be trying to occupy more space than they physically can—reaching out, rising to their full height, or spreading themselves wide as they turn.[21]

"You examine the natural, instinctive gesture," José said, "and find out how it can be translated, stylized or exaggerated to say what needs to be said with a fresh impact—immediately and powerfully—on many people. I don't like to play games with an audience—I always want them to know what's going on." The "impressive humanity"[22] of José's work was the result of such directness, and a manifestation of José's character:

[Limón] was always singularly lacking in a self-conscious concentration on self that many artists seem to need to survive. He had instead a remarkable warmth and sensitivity to others that made him perhaps the most personally beloved dancer of his generation. Certainly those who were touched by him—audiences, students, fellow-dancers—felt an affection for him that is an important part of his immortality.[23]

With the death of José Limón in 1972 members of his company faced the daunting task of regrouping under new leadership and continuing their work. I was acting artistic director until Ruth Currier and, later, Lucas Hoving took over the position, and with their able artistic advice the company managed to weather the loss of its founder. That the Limón Company now flourishes, under the direction of Carla Maxwell, is testimony not only to the faith and hard work of its members but to the real strength of José's leadership. As early as 1946, when the modern dance movement was still laboring in relative obscurity, its leading artists struggling to get reestablished after the enormous upheaval of the war years, José testified to his belief in the authenticity and durability of modern dance. The very existence of this book is a tribute to his foresight and that of other early exponents—a handful of visionaries who, collectively, created a new American art form:

The opinion is sometimes expressed that American dance will disappear along with its contemporary personalities when they retire from the stage. I do not believe this. The American dance has already known approximately three generations of artist exponents. Each generation has contributed to its impetus, its power and its expressiveness. This sort of dance is inevitable. It is actually compelled out of us by our great continent with its crude magnificences. It is not merely a style or idiom. It is a potent idea, and when contemporary personalities retire, the ideal will persist.[24]

Betty Jones and José Limón in The Moor's Pavane.

PART TWO

The Basics

The dancer is fortunate
indeed, for he has for
his instrument the most
eloquent and miraculous
of all instruments, the
human body.

JOSÉ LIMÓN, "ON DANCE"

*José Limón rehearsing the
"Feast of Harpies" from* The Winged,
*Palmer Auditorium,
Connecticut College (1966).*

The Limón Style

When he first began to choreograph his own pieces, José Limón brought to his work all the abandon of a twenty-year-old trying to find out what his body could and could not do. It was a raw style that came quite simply out of the process of his own discovery of dance, before he learned the technical "craft" of dancing; that is, before he learned how to point his feet or straighten his legs in the air. He threw himself into everything he did without worrying about balance, or shape, or what dancing was supposed to look like—and audiences were enchanted and excited by the daring, strength, virility and riskiness of his dancing. As he developed and studied more technique, he combined this daring and exuberance with the clarity of form and line made possible by greater muscular control. The results were, and still are, magical to watch.

John Martin wrote that "[Limón] has a magnificent body under superb control and is master of a prodigious technique. . . . His dance is that of a strong and mature man in command of all his powers, and it gives a completely new meaning and range to male dancing." After decades of thinking of male dancers simply as support posts for their female partners, this aspect of Limón's style—a further development of Ted Shawn's and Charles Weidman's breakthroughs—was important, and it enlarged the stylistic possibilities for both male and female dancers.

But Martin quickly put this aspect of José's style into perspective. Limón's interest, he said, did *not* lie "in the bravura that comes with jumps and turns." José's primary aesthetic and the more exciting aspect of his works was in "the transfer through movement of an awareness of heroic vision, of human experience, of poetic perception."[25] In his choreography, that heroic vision led José to sources in literature and historic events— Adam and Eve, Othello, the American Indian, the Poles after World War II—resonant, universal themes that reflected the full dimensions of the human experience. His dancers' turns, balances, lunges and soaring leaps seemed to be the irrepressible physical expression of the human spirit.

I danced with José Limón not because it was a job and I was a dancer, but because he brought me to a way of dancing that was as close to a spiritual experience as I ever had. I developed a tremendous sense of physical and spiritual unity that made me feel at one with my body and at the same time able to transcend its physical limitations. This was the result not only of José's aesthetic vision but also of more technical elements in his approach. Some of the most important concepts stemmed from his respect for the human body and his ability to use it to its fullest capacity without abusing or distorting it.

On stage, a Limón dancer seems to challenge the law of gravity—executing spiraling turns that appear almost to lift off the ground, the next minute lunging into a series of weighted, earth-bound runs, or balancing effortlessly on one leg as the body tilts to one side suspended in a completely off-balance position. But the effect is not one of weightlessness, as in ballet, of complete freedom from the pull of gravity. Describing a performance by the Limón Company, one critic observed that "one of the outstanding characteristics of modern dance is the use of gravity as a force. The floor is a strong base from which the dancer rises to great heights, only to return and rise again. The interplay of vertical movements is a breathing quality which infuses the dance with life itself."[26]

The Limón dancer continually confronts gravity, exploring the full spectrum of movement that exists between freedom from gravity and complete subservience to its power, between the moment of suspension just as the body is airborne and the moment the body falls or sinks to the earth—the range of movement Doris Humphrey called the "arc between two deaths."

Today professional and non-professional dancers alike come to Limón classes to study this unique quality of movement, a quality achieved by training the body in a specific "language" of movement, or style. Style determines *how* a movement or step is executed; that is, what muscle action achieves the movement, what the timing of the movement is and what kind of quality of expression is given to the movement.

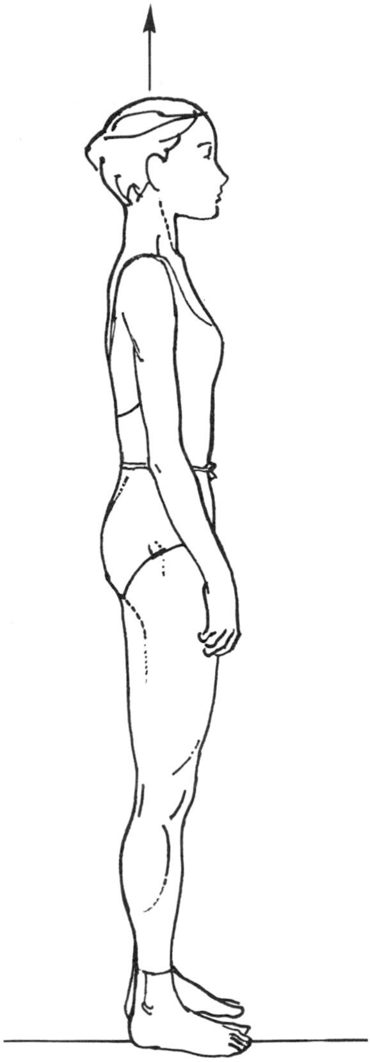

Illustration 1

Definitions and Preparatory Exercises

Before proceeding into class, I want to give you some idea of the basic concepts of movement that underlie the "language," or style, of Limón technique. Limón dancers learn to think about movement in terms of *alignment, succession, opposition, potential* and *kinetic energy, fall, weight, recovery* and *rebound*, and *suspension.* By implementing these principles in exercises, the dancer achieves the length, stretch and strength in the muscles that provide the freedom to do the swings, off-center turns, suspensions and other more difficult movements in the Limón technique. These concepts form the basic vocabulary of the Limón style, and it is the dancer's physical mastery of the vocabulary that makes the movement look expansive, effortless and free.

The following simple preparatory exercises will permit you to experience these principles in your own body and become familiar with them. Later, as you go through the class, you will employ these fundamentals again and again.

ALIGNMENT

Ordinarily, alignment refers to the placement of the feet, hips and shoulders in a standing position. But in fact alignment is the placement of *all* the parts of the body in relationship to each other. If you watch people walk down the street or stand in line, you will notice that each person's posture is different: some people lead with their head when they walk, some with their abdomen, some slouch or stand with all their weight on one hip. All of these attitudes in the body indicate incorrect alignment. Aside from looking awkward, incorrect alignment (bad posture) puts a strain on the spine and hinders graceful and efficient movement.

Look at yourself sideways in a mirror to check your own habitual posture. There should be a slight natural convex curve in the lower part of your spine (Illus. 1). However, if that curve is exaggerated so that your chest and abdomen protrude and your pelvis tilts back, your back is swayed and you are poorly aligned. If the curve is concave so that your lower back is rounded, your shoulders droop and your pelvis tilts forward, you are standing in a round-shouldered position and are poorly aligned. All spines have different degrees and types of curves. However, it is possible to align the whole body so that exaggerated curves in the spine are corrected and any stress on the spine caused by poor alignment is relieved.

When I talk about proper alignment, or placement, I am talking about a standing posture in which the feet are parallel (toes pointing forward) and placed directly under the hip joints (no wider than the hips). The shoulders are lined up over the hips (if you could drop a plumb line from the center of the shoulder, it would fall right through the center of the hip joint), the spine feels long, the head is lifted and the weight is evenly distributed between both feet. You should be able to sense your vertical axis. Imagine that a pole goes right through your body from a point between your feet through the center of the top of your head. This pole represents your vertical axis. When you lift from the top of your head, you lift from the point at which the pole, or axis, shoots up and out.

Very little muscle action is required to hold the body upright if it is properly aligned, so your muscles will be as relaxed as possible in this position. Once you discover how to align yourself properly in a standing position, you will find that you can move from it and return to it quickly and gracefully.

PREPARATORY EXERCISE: Stand with your feet directly below your hip joints, toes pointing forward. Let your arms hang loosely at your sides. Imagine that there is a headlight in each hip bone and that both headlights are shining straight forward. Your hips are now "square" to the front. Now imagine a straight line extending up from each hip bone to the shoulder above it. Your shoulders should be directly over your hips, and "square" to the front. Use the image of a headlight in each shoulder joint to help you "square off."

Rock from side to side to feel the weight move from one foot to other. Place your weight evenly on both feet. Now rock forward and back gently to feel the weight move back and forth between the toes and the heels. Try to distribute your weight evenly between the toes and the heels, right over your arches.

You are now properly aligned. Be sure that your muscles are relaxed,

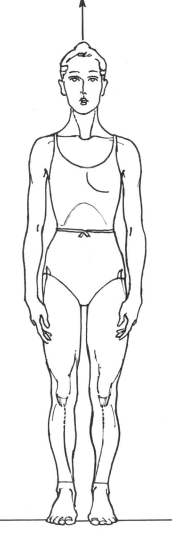

Illustration 2

not tensed. This position should feel easy and comfortable and you should have the sense that you are prepared to move in any direction.

Take a deep breath. Think of filling your head with helium, and begin to rise from the top of the head until your heels lift off the floor and you are in a high relevé. Try to feel as if the helium in your head is lifting your body so high that your legs just hang from your hips, rather than trying to push up into relevé from the feet. Go straight up without taking the body forward, and allow the heels to move forward slightly. Let the breath out slowly, hissing as you exhale, and slowly lower the heels back to the floor. Repeat the relevé, breathing normally, and try to create the same sensation of filling the body with air. As you lower your heels, think of leaving the head where it is, very lifted, and allow the heels to stretch toward the floor, lengthening the calves, thighs and spine. You should feel very tall (Illus. 2).

SUCCESSION

Succession is the sequential path of movement through the parts of the body. It operates like a chain reaction, or a wave traveling through the body, moving different parts. As you experience succession in the spine, you will discover how the spine connects the head, shoulders, chest, waist, and how all are connected to the hips. Once you understand this concept, you will see how the arms move from their connection with the spine and how they open and close sequentially.

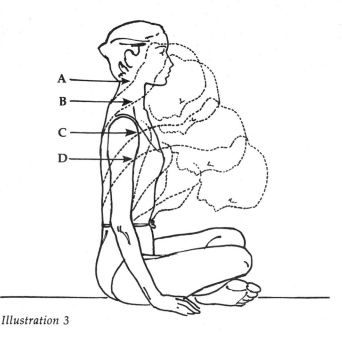

Illustration 3

PREPARATORY EXERCISES FOR SUCCESSIONAL FLOW IN THE SPINE: Start seated, with your legs crossed. Feel both "sit bones" *(ischia)* on the floor, spine vertical and stretched long, as if you were sitting with your back against a wall. Let your arms hang down by your sides, relaxed, with your hands resting on the floor. Focus front (Illus. 3, solid lines).

Take the top of your head forward and down toward the floor. Use the weight of your head to bring it down, keeping the muscles in your neck relaxed. As your head goes forward and down, think of keeping a lift in the neck (the cervical vertebrae) so that the head feels as if it is hanging from a "high point" in the center of the neck (Illus. 3, A).

As the spine starts to roll down, the high point will travel down the spine. Use the weight of the head to slowly keep the spine rolling down and allow just the shoulders to follow. Now the high point will be a little lower, right at the base of the neck (Illus. 3, B).

Keep the spine rolling down slowly, vertebra by vertebra, and allow the chest to follow. This begins to involve the thoracic vertebrae. The high point will be right between the shoulder blades (Illus. 3, C). As your spine rolls down, imagine that you are creating space between each of the vertebrae. Keep the arms and shoulders relaxed. Really feel as if your upper body is hanging comfortably from the high point.

Continue rolling down the spine and allow the waist (the lumbar vertebrae) to follow. Go as far as is comfortable. The high point will now be in the lower back (Illus. 3, D). When you have gone all the way over, feel how the weight of the head stretches the spine.

Now, beginning at the very base of your spine (think of the base of the spine as located right between the sit bones), slowly start to uncurl the spine back up to vertical. Remember the traveling high point, which is now in your lower back. Imagine that the high point is moving up the spine and bringing the spine up vertebra by vertebra—waist, chest, shoulders, neck and head. Try to maintain the feeling of space between the vertebrae as you uncurl. Feel the lift continue through the top of the head.

When you reach vertical, with the spine elongated and the top of the head reaching toward the ceiling, you will be at the peak of the movement. You have just completed the *successional* rolling down and up of the spine. Roll the spine down and back up several times, and try to feel the sequential path of the movement—head, shoulders, chest and waist.

In a side bend, the principle of the successional rolling down and up of the spine is the same. The only difference is that you are taking the spine down to the side rather than forward. From the same seated position, take the top of the head to the right and down toward the floor slowly, just as you did with the forward roll down—head, neck, shoulders, chest and waist (Illus. 4). Imagine the high point traveling slowly down the spine and try to maintain the sense of space between the vertebrae. This sense of space is particularly important in the side bend because it will help you to keep from sinking into your waist and feeling "crunched" in your side. Keep your

Illustration 4

shoulders and hips facing front as you go over and be sure to focus front. Your arms should be relaxed; you can slide your right hand along the floor beside you (Illus. 4). Feel how the weight of your head, as it reaches toward the floor, helps your spine to stretch.

Beginning at the base of the spine, roll the spine back up to vertical—waist, chest, shoulders, neck and head. Sense the stretch and elongation in your spine as the top of your head reaches toward the ceiling.

Practice the side bend several times to each side.

PREPARATORY EXERCISE FOR SUCCESSIONAL ARMS: For this exercise you may stand, properly aligned, or start seated, with your legs crossed. Beginning with the top of your head, successively roll your spine down. Keep your arms relaxed at your sides. Now, beginning at the base of your spine, start to uncurl the spine. As your chest lifts you will feel a slight pull in the shoulder blades. As soon as you feel this pull, allow it to bring your arms up, lower arms crossed, hugging your sides as if you were about to pull a sweater off over your head (Illus. 5). As the spine continues to uncurl and the shoulders relax, your elbows will rise until they are overhead with your lower arms crossed over each other. As your neck and head come to vertical, the chest will open (lift) slightly. At this point, feel how the opening in the chest brings the shoulder blades together in back, allowing the shoulders to fall into place. The action in the shoulders starts the elbows opening out to the sides and the arms extending on a high diagonal from the body (see Illus. 5 for the path of the arms). As your arms lengthen out to the sides—elbow, lower arm, wrist, hand—keep your hands flexed. This enables you to feel the stretch through the arms and along the upper back, helps to keep your shoulders relaxed and in place and activates the muscles along the ribs. Once you find the sensation of stretch and length in the arms and along the ribs, you can eliminate the flexed hands and do the successional arms with extended hands. However, be careful to keep the opposition

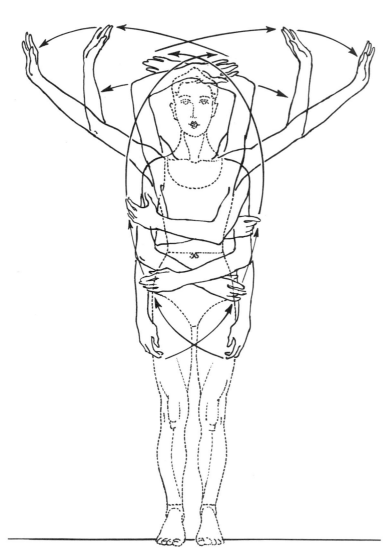

Illustration 5

going and the shoulders relaxed.

Think of succession in the arms as a chain reaction. The lift in the spine begins the process. As the chest and shoulders come to vertical the arms begin to rise; the opening of the chest and the lift in the neck and head allow the arms to open and extend out to the sides. Remember to lead with the lift in the body; the arms follow through as a result of the lift in the spine.

This chain of events is reversed as the spine starts to roll down. The rolling down of the head, neck and shoulders brings the hands, wrists, elbows and lower arms in toward the body. The arms cross and lower down to the sides as the rest of the spine curls down (see Illus. 5 and reverse the path of the arms).

Practice the successional opening and closing of the arms several times until you really sense the connection between the movement of the spine and the movement of the arms. Try to make the rolling down and rolling up of the spine and the opening and closing of the arms happen as smoothly and simultaneously as possible. Whenever I refer to successional arms later on in the exercises, I am referring to this sequence in the arms.

Now take the body into a side bend, rolling down and up succession-ally. This time only one arm will rise and open as the spine rolls up. As you take the body over to the right, allow the right arm to relax, resting the palm on the floor. As you roll the spine up to vertical, use the lift in the spine and the opening of the chest to bring the left arm up overhead and to open it out to the side. The action in the arm is exactly the same as in the forward successional roll: as the chest comes to vertical, the opening of the left side of the chest allows the left shoulder to fall into place and starts the arm opening out to the side. The chest continues to open as the arm extends: shoulder, elbow, wrist, palm, hand flexed. When you take the side bend to the left, the left arm will relax and the right arm will rise and open out successionally.

The successional arms I teach in these exercises are developed from the way Doris and José taught them. With José we did the successional arms just as I now teach them up to the point where the elbows are up over the head. Then we used to open the elbows out to the side and allow the rest of the arm to follow, opening out so the palms faced upward. Then, in order to help us feel suspension, he had us turn the palms down. When I began teaching I added the flexed hands to help stretch the arms out, drop the ribcage and to keep the shoulders in place.

OPPOSITION

Opposition is a way of using the entire body to create the feeling of length and stretch in a movement, without tensing or gripping ("shortening") the muscles.

There are five points of opposition in the standing body: the head, the left hand, the right hand, the left foot, the right foot. If you think of a string attached to each of these points—one to the palm of each hand, one to the top of the head, one to the bottom of each foot—and imagine an equal pull outward on each string, you should feel very long and stretched in all your limbs and in your spine (Illus. 6).

Each of these five points of opposition in the extremities can oppose each of the others (Illus. 7). For example, think of a line drawn from the top of the head, down through the chest and out along the arm to the hand; now think of the two ends of the line (head and hand) stretching outward. This is the opposition between the top of the head and the hand. In other words, you can think of the right hand opposing the top of the head, the left hand opposing the top of the head, the right foot opposing the top of the head, the left foot opposing the top of the head, and so forth. If, for example, you are rolling the spine up to vertical and opening the arms out successionally, as in the previous exercise, you can use the oppositional pulls to help you get the stretch and length in the arms and in the spine. As the arms lengthen, think of the opposition of the right hand to the top of the head and the opposition of the left hand to the top of the head and use these oppositions to help you feel the connection of the arms to each other and how they relate to the lift in the spine.

As you experienced the successional rolling down and up of the spine, you used the top of the head and the base of the spine as points from which the movement began

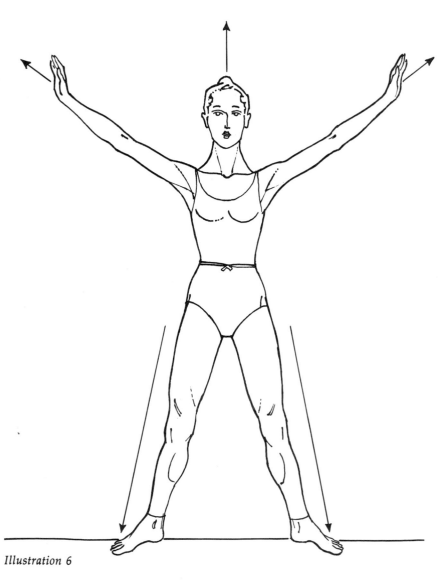

Illustration 6

and as points from which to lengthen. The traveling high point in the spine helped you feel how the lift moved up and down the vertebrae. The traveling high point is what we call the sixth oppositional point in the body, and it comes into play as the body begins to move. This sixth oppositional point in the spine is always moving as the body moves, just as it moves throughout the succession in the spine.

POTENTIAL AND KINETIC ENERGY

Energy is the capacity of the body to move, and *potential* energy is that capacity in its unreleased state, that is, the body on the threshold of movement. *Kinetic* energy is potential energy in motion.

In the context of this technique, by potential energy we mean energy that is stored in the body and can be released through gravity. When this energy is released, it becomes kinetic energy. The simplest example of this transformation of energy is a fall. You will learn how to harness this energy by sensing the potential energy in different parts of the body and discovering how to release it in order to create momentum.

FALL

A fall is the complete release of the muscles as the body, giving in to gravity, drops. In the context of Limón technique, you will learn how to let different parts of the body fall independently. For example, your head, shoulders and chest can fall forward while your waist, hips and legs remain upright. A fall in any part of the body, as well as in the entire body, releases a vast amount of kinetic energy. This energy can be harnessed by catching it in either a recovery or a rebound.

The principles of physics state that in a vacuum any object will fall at a rate of 32 feet per second per second. This means that it accelerates more every second as it falls toward the floor. Imagine the body falling in

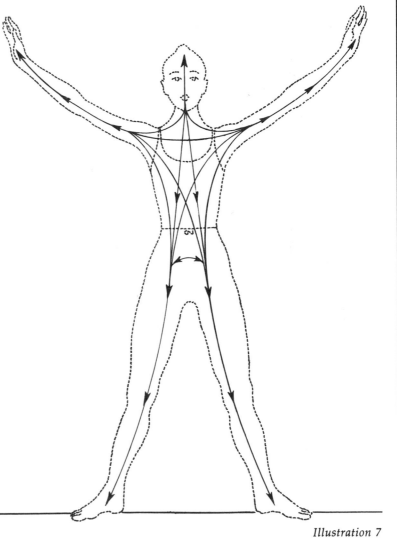

Illustration 7

a vacuum at an ever-increasing rate of speed, so that it falls ever more rapidly—rather than at a steady pace—toward the floor. This image can be used for a fall in any part of the body.

WEIGHT

The use of weight is the hardest element of Limón technique to define and apply because it is itself a quality of movement. Within a technical aspect of a movement, such as opposition or suspension, weight is added by isolating a part of the body and allowing it to succumb to gravity while maintaining the suspensions, oppositions and high points in the rest of the body.

RECOVERY AND REBOUND

The end result of recovery and rebound is the same: the potential energy released in a fall is accumulated at the bottom of the fall and rechanneled. In a *recovery*, the energy passes through the bottom of the fall and continues in the same path, like the swing of a pendulum. The energy continues along the lines of centrifugal force. In a *rebound*, it is the elastic reaction of the muscles that is utilized. When a part of the body falls, the muscles will reach the limit of their stretch at the bottom of the fall and naturally pull back or contract slightly, like a spring. In a rebound this regathered energy is shunted into a new direction.

SUSPENSION

A suspension is a prolonged high point. It is created at the peak of the movement by continuing the movement and delaying the takeover of gravity.

A suspension is a heightening of potential energy—a "breath"—at the peak of the movement. When you take a breath, the body fills with air and the oppositional pulls between head, hands and feet elongate, or extend. You are trying to create this feeling of breath, without actually taking a deep breath, at the suspended moment. By suspending a movement at its high point you create both the internal and external impression that the body is floating.

PREPARATORY EXERCISE FOR ALIGNMENT, FALL AND REBOUND IN THE KNEES: This exercise is designed to illustrate the principle of alignment and to help you understand how the combination of the weight of the head in the fall, the elasticity of the spine and the release in the knees creates the feeling of rebound throughout the entire body.

Stand and align your body as in the exercise for alignment: shoulders over hips, hips and shoulders square to the front, feet at hip width with toes pointed forward. Let your arms hang loosely at your sides (Illus. 8, solid lines). Take a deep breath. Think of filling your head with helium and begin to rise from the top of the head until your heels lift off the floor and you are in a high relevé. Try to feel as if the helium in your head is lifting your body so high that your legs just hang from your hips, rather than as if you were pushing up into the relevé from your feet. Let the breath out slowly, hissing as you exhale, and slowly lower the heels back to the floor. Repeat the relevé, breathing normally, and try to create the same sensation of filling with air. As you lower your heels, think of leaving the head where it is, very lifted, and allow the heels to stretch toward the floor, lengthening the calves, thighs and spine. You should feel very tall and properly aligned.

Take the top of your head forward and down, without letting your shoulders go (Illus. 8, A). Feel the high point right in the center of your neck; imagine a string attached to the high point, lifting upward. If you really let the weight of your head go over, the natural stretch in the neck muscles will cause a slight rebound, or bounce. Let your head bounce 4 times to a waltz rhythm: $\overset{>}{1}$ 2 3 / $\overset{>}{2}$ 2 3 / $\overset{>}{3}$ 2 3 / $\overset{>}{4}$ 2 3, bouncing on the first beat in each measure. (Bounce on the count of $\overset{>}{1}$, rebound slightly on the – 2 3, bounce on count $\overset{>}{2}$, rebound slightly on counts – 2 3, and so forth.)

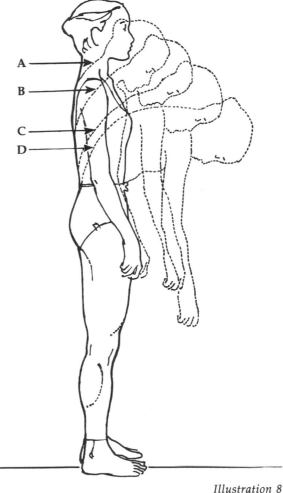

Now allow the weight of your head to take your shoulders over with it. Bounce 4 more times with the head and the shoulders, using the same waltz rhythm. This time the high point will be right at the base of your neck (Illus. 8, B). Maintain the lift in the high point as you bounce.

Add the chest, letting your arms hang loosely. Bounce 4 times with the head, shoulders and chest. The high point is now right between your shoulder blades (Illus. 8, C).

Allow as much of your waist to go over as is comfortable. Keep your hips in place. Bounce 4 times with the head, shoulders, chest and waist. The high point will now be in the lower back (lumbar) (Illus. 8, D).

Add a slight bend in the knees and try to feel the rebound action in the knees as you bounce 4 times from the high point in your lower back (Illus. 9). Keep your arms relaxed and loose.

Deepen the bend in the knees and take 4 more bounces, keeping the body over and the high point lifting. Take 1 more bounce (the fifth bounce) and use the rebound of that bounce to begin to lift the spine successively up to

Illustration 8

vertical. As the high point travels up the spine, each part (waist, chest, shoulders, head) will come to vertical in turn, and the lift in the body from the high point will allow the legs to straighten. Take 4 counts to accomplish the lift to vertical. You should now be standing in the position in which you began: feet underneath the hips, hips and shoulders square to the front, top of the head lifting toward the ceiling.

Lift into relevé (as you did at the beginning of this exercise—remember the feeling of filling your head with helium) in 2 counts and lower the heels in 2 counts.

It is a good idea to check your alignment with your knees bent and your head, shoulders, chest and waist over forward, to be sure you are getting the proper stretch in the spine and accomplishing the rebound correctly. Stand tall, properly aligned, as you did at the beginning of the exercise. Take your head, shoulders, chest and waist over forward, bend your knees slightly and let your arms hang at your sides. Your head should feel very heavy, the top of the head reaching toward the floor. Ask someone to place his hand on your upper back, between your shoulder blades, and gently push, bouncing up and down like a ball. You should be able to feel the stretch and rebound in the spine. This is the movement you are trying to achieve as you accomplish the exercise.

Now try the entire exercise with a side bend, taking the head, the shoulders, chest and waist over to the right in stages, 4 bounces at a time (Illus. 10). Finish with 4 bounces, adding the knees. Be sure to keep your focus to the front throughout the exercise. It will be a little harder to feel as much of a rebound in the side bend as you did in the fall forward, because your body naturally bends over farther to the front. Try to create the same feeling of rebound and remember to feel the traveling high point.

Now try the entire exercise to the left side.

PREPARATORY EXERCISE #1 FOR FALL AND REBOUND IN THE LEGS: This exercise is designed to help you experience the feeling of fall and rebound in the legs. Although I do not teach this exercise in every class, I use it when a class is having difficulty really experiencing the rebound and resilience in the legs.

Stand in second position, arms hanging loosely at your sides.

Drop into a plié in second position, knees pointing out over your toes. (It is very important that your knees point out directly over your toes, rather than behind or in front of them. Aligning your knees properly will allow the knee mobility and will prevent strain.) Let your arms hang down in

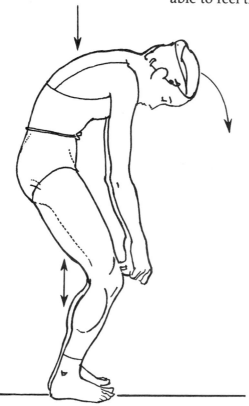

Illustration 9

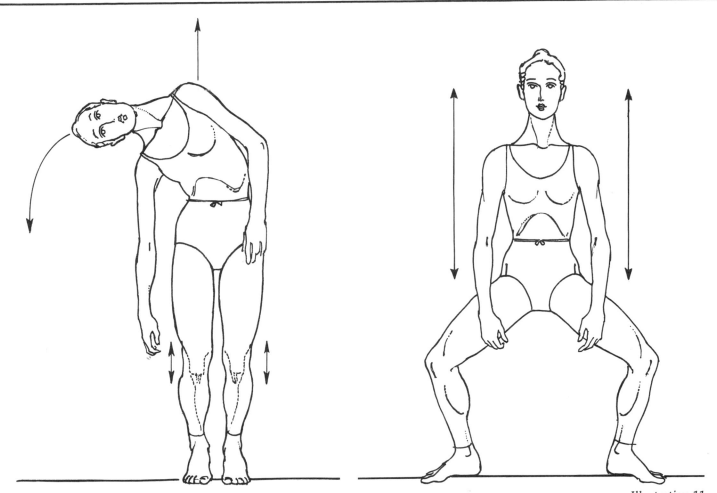

Illustration 10

Illustration 11

front of you (Illus. 11). Feel the stretch in your legs in the plié, and allow the legs to rebound; this is the same rebound that you felt in your knees in the first rebound exercise. The addition of the stretch of second position gives the rebound a little more energy.

This exercise is a series of 8-count phrases at a medium tempo. Bounce 5 times, counting 1 2 3 4 5, with a little more rebound in each bounce. On the fifth bounce use the energy of the rebound and a lift in your body to bring the body up on the counts of 6 7 8, so the legs can straighten. Make sure to maintain a feeling of opposition between the top of the head and the base of the spine as you bounce (see the arrows in Illus. 11). This will help you keep the lift going in the torso so that it will ride freely on top of the legs. The hips and the spine should not feel as if they are pulling or pushing each other; they should be moving as a unit.

If you are having difficulty feeling the speed of the drop, keep the lift going on counts 6 7 8 up into a relevé so that you will have a greater distance to drop when you begin again. This drop is a fall, which is then redirected by a rebound.

Repeat these bounces 2 to 4 times.

Illustration 12

Illustration 13

PREPARATORY EXERCISE #2 FOR FALL AND REBOUND IN THE LEGS: In this exercise you will use the same fall and rebound in second position as in the previous exercise. The difference here is that the little bounces have been taken out and the meter has been changed to a waltz rhythm: $\overset{>}{1}$ 2 3 / $\overset{>}{2}$ 2 3 / $\overset{>}{3}$ 2 3 / $\overset{>}{4}$ 2 3 / and so forth. Use a medium tempo.

Start in second position. Drop into a plié on count 1, rebound and rise on counts – 2 3. Repeat 4 times, until you feel the fall and the rebound happening naturally, almost without conscious effort. As you arrive at the top, take a breath in order to suspend the movement for just a moment.

On the fourth rebound, as your legs straighten, take the counts of − 2 3 to lift your arms overhead, as if you were pulling off a sweater. Leave the arms overhead as you begin the next sequence of pliés.

Repeat the pliés in second position 4 more times, adding the arms as follows: Drop into a plié and let the arms swing down in front of you, crossing at the wrists as they fall (Illus. 12, dotted lines). As you rebound and lift to straighten the legs, let the arms swing out to the sides up to shoulder height (Illus. 13).

Again drop into a plié and let the arms swing down in front of you, crossing at the wrists. As you rebound and lift to straighten the legs, bring your arms up in front of you and overhead, as in the beginning position (pulling off a sweater).

Note: Though you will do 4 pliés, you will do only 2 complete arm sequences. If you are having difficulty feeling the speed of the drop, keep the lift going on counts 6 7 8 up into a relevé and suspend the relevé so that you will have a greater distance to drop when you begin again.

Repeat 4 more times, with the legs and arms the same. On the next count of 1, drop into a plié and take a side bend to the right with the plié; the arms swing down and cross at the wrists (Illus. 14, solid lines). Keep the focus front. On counts − 2 3, lift in the body (the high point is now in the rib-cage) to straighten the legs. The arms swing out to the sides, to shoulder height (dotted lines). The body stays over to the side, and as the legs straighten the head goes over farther toward the floor.

On the first count of the second measure, drop into a plié and drop the arms down in front of you (Illus. 15, solid lines). Lift on the counts of − 2 3, to bring the body back up to vertical and to straighten the legs. As you lift, bring the arms up in front of you, crossing at the wrists (Illus. 15, dotted lines). Let the high point travel up from the ribcage to the top of the head as you come to vertical.

Repeat to the left.

You can keep the lift going into a relevé each time you lift to straighten the legs, so that you will have a greater distance to drop

Illustration 14

when you begin again. The moment just before you drop is a good time to practice feeling the suspension. As you relevé with the body in a side bend, remember to feel the high point in the ribcage.

PREPARATORY EXERCISE FOR THE HANDS: During a class, tension in the body often manifests itself in the hands. When José saw this tension building during class, he would often stop us and give a lecture on the use and importance of the hand. He would say, "The hand is the seal upon the deed. A powerful gesture with the body cannot fully convince unless the hand is in accord with it." He would then spend a few minutes describing what our hands looked like: lobster claw hands, hands dipped in hot oil, or veal cutlet hands. All very different, none right. He tried to get the breath into our hands with the following exercise, which can be done at any time during a class or as a preparatory exercise.

You can do this either standing or sitting, whichever is more comfortable. Touch your fingertips together in front of your chest, palms down, elbows bent and out to the sides. Drop your pinkies down and lift your thumbs up, stretching and spreading the fingers out as far as you can without turning the wrists. When you can go no farther, bring the elbows down and in toward each other so the palms of the hands turn up and out, presenting the palms forward (Illus. 16, solid lines). Relax the hands. Lift the elbows to the sides so that the palms rotate down and the fingertips are touching, as in the opening position (Illus. 16, dotted lines).

Continue opening the arms out to the sides, leading with the elbows, followed by the wrists and then the hands, until the arms are stretched out to the sides at shoulder height with the palms down, fingers together. Drop the pinkies down, lift the thumbs and spread the fingers out. When you cannot go any farther with the fingers, drop the elbows down slightly in order to allow the wrists to rotate so that the palms turn up (Illus. 17, solid lines). Reverse by relaxing the fingers, lifting the elbows, rotating the wrists and turning the palms over. Leading with the wrists (Illus. 17, insert), draw the hands in and bring the fingertips together, back to the opening position (Illus. 16, dotted lines).

Variation: Try taking one arm up and the other out to the side in the second part of the exercise; then reverse which arm goes up and which one goes out to the side.

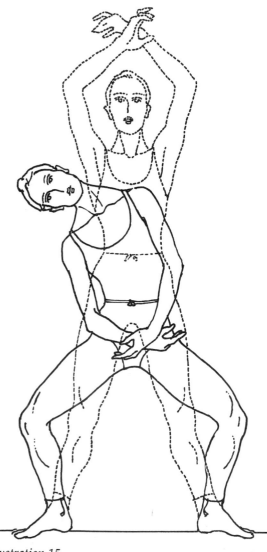

Illustration 15

ISOLATIONS

José always gave the following isolations at the beginning of class. Once we understood each separate isolation, we would then work on connecting them. I use these exercises when teaching beginners so they can experience isolating different parts of the body without having to worry about balance or placement.

PREPARATORY EXERCISES FOR ISOLATIONS: These exercises are done lying on your back on the floor. Stretch your legs out in front of you and stretch your arms out to the sides, resting on the floor at about shoulder height, palms down. Rotate the hip joints so that the entire leg "turns out"; the knees are pointing away from each other instead of up to the ceiling, the inner thighs and calves are touching, the heels are touching, and the sides of the feet are resting on the floor. Keep your legs in this position during the following exercises.

Rib and Elbow Isolation: From the starting position on the floor, take a side bend to the right. Allow the right elbow to draw in along the floor toward the ribs, palm turning up (Illus. 18, A). Straighten the body and allow the elbow to rotate along the floor, so that the hand and fore-

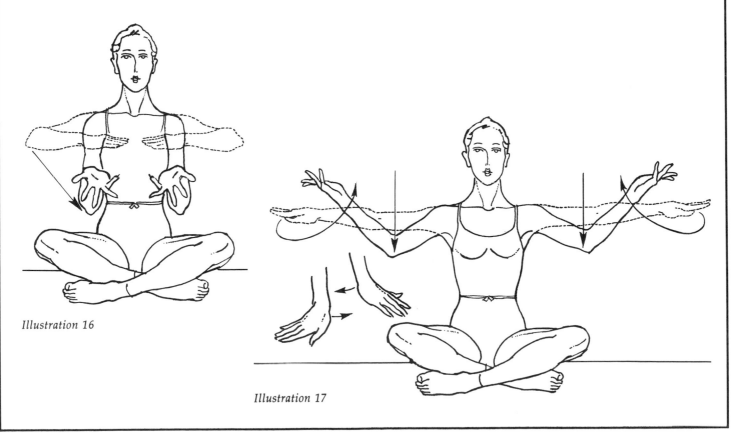

Illustration 16

Illustration 17

arm turn over and the palm is down. Stretch the arm out to the side (Illus. 18, B). Repeat to the left side. Connect all the movements so that the side bend initiates the movement of the elbow and arm. Be sure to keep the hips in place so that the movement in the body is isolated in the ribcage.

Elbow and Shoulder Isolation: Lying on your back, arms out to the sides, bring your right elbow in toward your ribs. Relax your hand and wrist, allowing the palm to turn up (Illus. 19, A). When the elbow reaches the ribs, rotate the right shoulder in toward the chest, which will bring the elbow up off the floor (Illus. 19, B). Allow the elbow to continue to reach toward the ceiling, followed by the lower arm, the wrist and the hand. The whole right arm should be stretched upward and the wrist should be rotated so that the palm faces away from the body (Illus. 19, C).

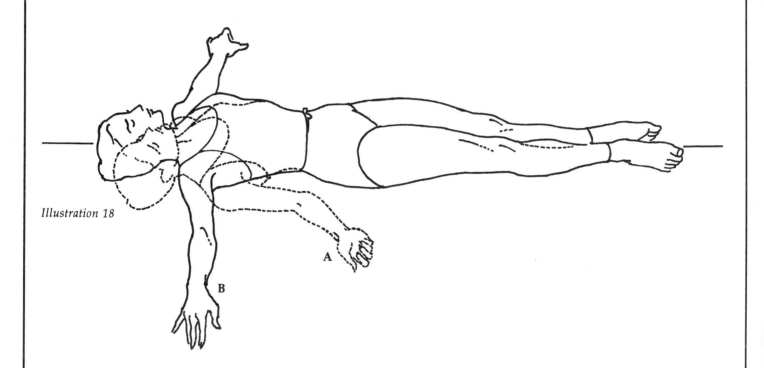

Illustration 18

Reverse the entire process by starting with shoulder and rotating it back down to the floor. Keep the arm stretched, with a feeling of opposition in the hand, so that the arm does not simply drop down. Pull the elbow down and in toward the ribs, lift it out to the side along the floor, and stretch the rest of the arm along the floor until it is lengthened out to the side. Try this with the left arm and practice the exercise with each arm until it can be done smoothly and comfortably.

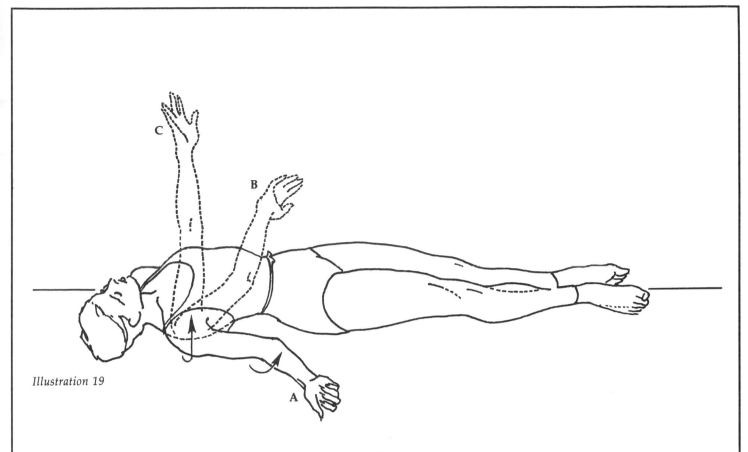

Illustration 19

Chest Isolation: Arch your back as high as it will go, leaving the top of your head, your arms and your pelvis on the floor (Illus. 20). Then lower your spine to the floor, starting with the lumbar and allowing the spine to relax to the floor vertebra by vertebra. Your pelvis will tuck as you lower the spine.

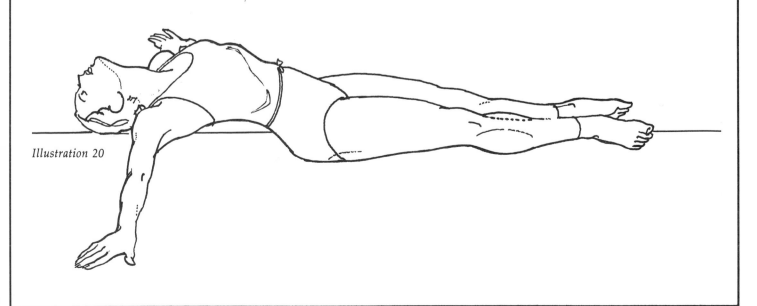

Illustration 20

These isolations can be combined in different ways. Add the Elbow and Shoulder Isolation to the Chest Isolation, moving both arms at the same time. The chest arches, the elbows draw in, the shoulders rotate in and the arms straighten up. The top of the head will support the body weight in the arch so that the arms and shoulders are free to move. Reverse the arms: bring the shoulders down and the elbows down and in toward the ribs. Then lower the chest. Finally, stretch the arms out to the sides along the floor. Try to find a connection between the movements by sensing how one causes the next to happen.

Add the side bend from the Rib and Elbow Isolation to the Elbow and Shoulder Isolation. As the body bends to the side, the elbow draws in, the shoulder rotates and the arm extends. Then reverse the arm movement, keeping the side bend. Rotate and lower the shoulder back to the floor and draw the elbow down and in toward the ribs. Straighten the body and rotate the elbow along the floor as you stretch the arm out to the side.

Remember to feel the oppositional pulls in the body as you do the isolation exercises.

NOTES TO TEACHERS

I've included specific notes for teachers for each exercise in Part Three, but here I want to describe the overall picture of the class and how it is conducted.

I try to create a pleasant working atmosphere during the hour and a half to two hours of class, without losing the discipline of the teacher-student relationship. I think of myself not so much as a teacher but as an artist, sharing my knowledge with other artists. My students are always teaching me as well, by sharing their fresh ideas, new images and individual approaches while I guide them through the process of learning and discovery. By asking students to correct each other, I make them part of the teaching process, and I find that they often learn faster through the practical experience of seeing someone else's difficulties and helping to correct them.

One technique that I use and that I have students use when correcting each other is to find a visual image for the movement. This helps to define for the student the quality, shape, rhythm and overall pattern in the body. Images can be either internal or external. To create an internal image, such as feeling the opposition between two points in the body, find the path of the movement in the muscles and how they connect. Then find an image that expresses that connection within the body: the spine as an elastic band stretching between the top of the head and the base of the spine, for example. This illustrates the connection and gives it a definite quality. An external image serves to clarify the body's path through space.

In any exercise where the body passes from a side bend toward one side of the body through vertical to a side bend toward the other side, try using the image of a rainbow arcing overhead. One of the colors is missing from the rainbow and there is a paintbrush filled with that color on top of the dancer's head. As the body goes from one side to the other, the paint brush must paint the missing color along the arc of the rainbow. This image helps to keep the top of the head stretching out into space so that the body makes a complete arc in the movement. These images are used only to experience the movement the first time. Once the student has found and achieved the movement correctly, muscle memory should take over and the image will no longer be needed. One image will not always work for every student, so encourage them to come up with their own.

Although I have eliminated the barre as part of my class, I find it a useful teaching aid for students having difficulty getting the quality of a movement. I will bring them to the barre and isolate that portion of the movement that is giving them trouble. For example, the student must avoid pushing himself up into relevé using only his feet and legs; instead, he should use the lift in the high point as he comes out of the side bend to lift him into relevé. At the barre the student can work on the feeling of lift without having to worry about balancing. When they are secure with the movement at the barre, I bring them back out to the center of the floor.

José Limón teaching class at the Juilliard School of Music.

PART THREE

The Class

[Dance is] an art that
literally epitomizes
the old bromide about
"honest sweat." . . . For
muscles never stay
stretched, you know.
One good painful
stretching on Monday
will not do for Tuesday.
Tuesday will demand its
share of the discomforts,
as well as Wednesday
and Thursday and the
rest of the week.
. . . Sweat, you know, is
for most sensible human
beings not quite nice.
Not quite delicate,
nor mannerly, and to be
avoided wherever
possible. But a dancer
lives—I use this verb
in all its implications
and with all emphasis—
lives in it, with it,
around it, soaked with it,
permeated by it,
marinated in it.

—JOSÉ LIMÓN, "ON MAGIC"

About Counts, Meter, Phrasing and Tempo

In class dancers work to warm up the body, to build stamina and strength and to learn technique. A class can run from an hour and a half to two hours and always comprises a series of exercises. We start with simple warm-up exercises, but once the muscles are warm and supple, the exercises become more demanding and complex.

We begin with exercises performed from a seated position and proceed to exercises done standing and then those that move across the floor. The following exercises are those I teach in my classes and which I feel are basic to an understanding of Limón technique. Each of the exercises is divided into three levels: elementary, intermediate and advanced.

The exercises at the elementary level serve to introduce the nondancer to Limón technique and train the dancer in its most basic principles. The technique does not require a great deal of physical effort, because it focuses on the simple use of body weight and relaxed muscles to accomplish the stretches, rather than on pushing, pulling or forcing the muscles to stretch. Once you are familiar with the exercises you can vary their order and combination to create a series that suits your own body.

The intermediate exercises are designed for those who have had some basic ballet or modern dance training. However, you must master the elementary level of each exercise before attempting the intermediate, as the intermediate version assumes that you are familiar enough with the basic mechanics to add on stylist variations.

The advanced section is designed only for those who are professional dancers, serious dance students, or teachers. You must be comfortable at the intermediate level of each exercise before going on to the advanced.

This is particularly important when doing advanced versions in which there are turns; you must master the basics of the exercise in order to successfully add the turns. (Labanotation—a method of notating dance movement, analogous to music notation—is included in the Appendix for the advanced exercises, as well as for the variations, so that teachers can use elements of the advanced version of work across the floor for creating other variations on the exercises. Some Labanotation is included for the basics as well, for use by advanced students and teachers.)

In order to describe or teach a movement or exercise, I break it down by "counting" it. The counts tell you in what sequence a certain motion or series of motions should be executed.

Occasionally as I am describing an exercise, I subdivide the counts by adding an "and" (&) count between two counts: 1 & 2 & 3 & 4 & and so forth. This is done to help you find where you are in the movement, halfway between two counts.

Before each exercise you will find a description of the meter, tempo and phrasing:

METER: 3/4
TEMPO: medium, and a little faster

PHRASING: 1 2 3/ 2 2 3/ 3 2 3/ 4 2 3/ 5 2 3/ 6 2 3/ 7 2 3/ 8 2 3

Meter is the organization of counts, or beats, by measures. Measures are, simply, groups of counts or beats. In the example above, the division of counts into measures is indicated by the slashes in the phrasing. The first count of each measure indicates which measure it is. If the counts read /3 2 3/, for example, you are in the third measure.

In musical terms a meter of 3/4 indicates three quarter notes, or beats, per measure, each quarter note representing one beat. A waltz, for example, is in a meter of 3/4.

Tempo is the hardest element of movement to get across on the printed page. Even dancers and musicians rehearsing together often find that each has a different concept of what the tempo should be for the same piece of music. Frequently they must submit to an independent arbiter—the metronome. The metronome provides the only "scientific" way of getting everyone to agree on the same tempo. The metronome is set to tick a certain number of beats per minute. A setting of 60 would be 60 beats per minute, or one beat per second. This is what I consider a *medium* tempo. A *fast* tempo would be twice as fast, or two beats per second (a metronome setting of 120), and a *slow* tempo would be one beat every two seconds (a metronome setting of 30). I have included precise metronome markings in the Notes to Teachers and tempo indications of fast, medium or slow with each exercise. You may vary the tempo of a given exercise to suit your body and your proficiency. You will find, however, that slower is not always easier.

The curved lines above the numbers indicate the *phrasing* and the > marks indicate accented counts. Phrasing tells you where to punctuate the movement by showing which series of movements are connected, much the way a comma groups words within a sentence. The accent marks show which are the stronger beats. Phrasing combined with accents creates the dynamics, or what I call the movement's "breath" (not literally the dancer breathing in and out, but the "breath" of the movement itself).

When I talk about phrasing, I am always referring to the phrasing of the movement, not the phrasing of the musical accompaniment (which appears at the end of each exercise in the Notes to Teachers).

The Notes to Teachers that conclude each exercise offer some teaching techniques designed to help students find the quality of the movement, as well as information on tempo and phrasing for musical accompaniment.

Floor Exercises

ONE: SPINAL SUCCESSION

PURPOSE: To warm up the spine in the sitting position and to stretch the legs.

José used to teach these as spine isolations: lying on the back on the floor, arching up to a sitting position and curling the spine back down to the floor (see the preparatory exercises for isolations in the preceding chapter). Arms, side bends, and bends in the legs were then added. I teach them in sitting position, however, because I have found that this is better for the alignment of the lower back.

METER: 4/4
TEMPO: slow

PHRASING: 1 2 3 4 / 5 6 7 8

OPENING POSITION: Sit up straight, shoulders over hips, knees bent with the soles of the feet on the floor. Keep the legs parallel. Arms can be wrapped around the knees or palms can rest flat on the floor for support (Illus. 1, solid lines).

PREPARATION (ALL LEVELS): Take a deep breath and exhale, hissing as you breathe out (make an "S" sound as you expel the breath so that the exhalation is even and so the ribcage drops), and allow the lower (lumbar) spine to round and sink back while the shoulders sink straight down. The body should feel completely relaxed (Illus. 1, dotted lines). Then slowly bring the spine up to vertical, starting with the lumbar, inhaling as you straighten the back.

Always begin sinking or straightening at the base of the spine—the lumbar—and continue up through the spine through the neck. Try the preparation with an exaggerated breath in and out once to

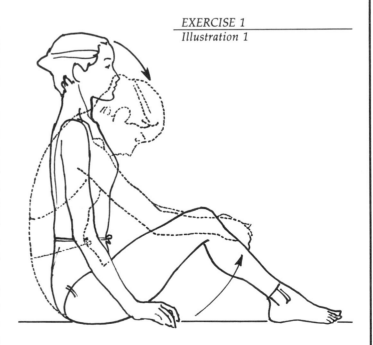

EXERCISE 1
Illustration 1

get the feel of it. Then repeat it with normal breathing, trying to re-create the feeling of the exaggerated breath. Take 4 counts to exhale and sink and 4 counts to inhale and straighten. Repeat at least 4 times.

ELEMENTARY

Counts 1 2 3 4: Start from the rounded position (the dotted lines in Illus. 1). Beginning at the base of the spine (lumbar), successively roll up the spine while extending the legs forward along the floor. Keep the soles of the feet sliding along the floor as long as possible and keep the toes pointed as the legs straighten. Continue until the spine is vertical and the legs are stretched out in front of you.

Counts 5 6 7 8: Beginning at the base of the spine (lumbar), reverse the whole process, bringing the feet in toward you and bending the knees as the spine releases and sinks.

SEQUENCE: Repeat the entire exercise 4 times: 4 counts up, 4 counts down.

INTERMEDIATE

The intermediate version is the same as the elementary, with the addition of an arch in the spine and flexed feet.

Counts 1 2 3: Beginning from the rounded position, successively roll up the spine as you extend the legs, exactly as in the elementary version, but accomplish the entire roll up in 3 counts.

Count 4: On the fourth count, keep the lift in the spine going and take the upper body into an arch, leading with the head, followed by the shoulders and the chest. At the same time, flex the feet. Arms are down at the sides (Illus. 2, solid lines).

Counts 5 6 7 8: Reverse, exactly as in the elementary version. On count 5 bring the upper body to vertical from the arch, then allow the spine to sink. Sink back to the rounded position in the last 3 counts.

SEQUENCE: Repeat the entire exercise 4 times: 4 counts up, 4 counts down.

ADVANCED

This is the same as the intermediate version, with the addition of arms.

Counts 1 2 3: Begin from the rounded position, arms wrapped around the knees. Start successively rolling the spine up and extending the legs, toes pointed. The arms will slide up along the legs toward your lap. The lower back (lumbar) will come to vertical, and the middle back (thoracic) will follow. As the thoracic comes to vertical, allow the arms to cross and rise, hugging the body (as if you were pulling a sweater off over your head) until the elbows are directly over your head. The spine should be vertical and the elbows overhead on the count of 3.

Count 4: Continue the lift into an arch in the upper body. The chest will open and the shoulders will fall into place. This causes the elbows to begin to open to the sides. The arms continue to extend and the hands flex (Illus. 2, dotted lines). This is the same sequential opening of the arms that you practiced in the Preparatory Exercise for Successional Arms. At the same time, flex the feet.

Counts 5 6 7 8: Reverse, as in the intermediate version, bringing the arms down toward the knees as the spine sinks and the legs draw in, back to the rounded position.

Try checking yourself once using an exaggerated breath, just to feel the lengthening in the spine. Then try to re-create the feeling with normal breathing.

Accomplish this exercise without any tension or tightening in the muscles. Feel the stretch and reaching of all the oppositional points. The torso should feel as if it is expanding in all directions as the spine uncurls, and the back of the legs should feel lengthening along the floor as they extend.

Try to keep the quality of the movement smooth and sustained throughout the exercise.

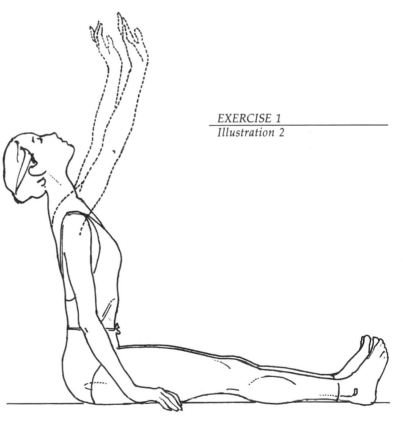

EXERCISE 1
Illustration 2

SEQUENCE: Repeat the entire exercise 4 times: 4 counts up, 4 counts down.

ADVANCED VARIATIONS

FIRST VARIATION: Try changing the counts. Repeat the exercise:
    4 times: 4 counts up, 4 counts down, then
    2 times: 3 counts up, 1 count down, then
    2 times: 1 count up, 3 counts down, then
    4 times: 1 count up, 1 count down.

The last 4 times the tempo can be slowed down to accommodate the movement.

Be sure that the quality of the movement does not change as the counts change. Keep it smooth and flowing, without jerks or stops. The first few times you do the exercise, do it slowly. As you become more familiar with it over time, gradually increase the tempo to a comfortable speed.

SECOND VARIATION: Using the counts of the original exercise (4 counts up, 4 counts down), add a twist in the spine and straighten each leg alternately. As you roll up, twist the spine to the right, arching on 4, and simultaneously lengthen the left leg along the floor. The right knee stays bent. Repeat to the left, twisting the spine to the left as you roll up and lengthening the right leg, keeping the left knee bent.

NOTES TO TEACHERS

The hardest thing to accomplish in this exercise is the quality of breathing in on the "up" and out on the "down," without actually taking big breaths. One way to find this quality is to have the student try to reverse the breathing, by breathing out on the "up" and in on the "down." The object is to give the illusion in the body of breathing in though the breath is actually going out.

Labanotation for this exercise is provided on page 188.

The metronome setting for this exercise is ♩ = 58 to 63
Phrasing for musical accompaniment:

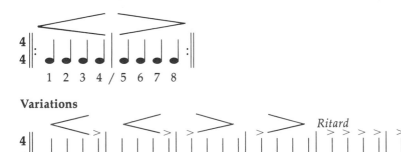

Variations

TWO: BOUNCES

PURPOSE: To warm up the spine. The goal is to discover how to use gravity, rather than the muscles, to do the work. Tension in the body prevents the stretch and release that you need in order to warm up the muscles; relaxed muscles release more easily. Bounces should in no way be forced: go as far as is comfortable for your body. Each position of the legs puts a different stretch on the spine.

These bounces are basically the same as those taught by Doris Humphrey, Charles Weidman and José Limón except that Doris and Charles originally taught them with the arms ending overhead and slightly open to the sides. José extended the arms into a V shape, and I have added a flexed hand to the V-shaped arms to help pull the shoulders down, activate the muscles along the ribs and help you feel the opposition between the two hands.

METER: 3/4
TEMPO: medium, and a little faster

PHRASING: 1̇ 2 3 / 2̇ 2 3 / 3̇ 2 3 / 4̇ 2 3 /

5̇ 2 3 / 6 2 3 / 7 2 3 / 8 2 3

OPENING POSITION: Sitting, soles of the feet together. Make a comfortable diamond shape with the legs and feet. The feet should not be too close to the body. The hands should rest comfortably on the floor, palms down, near your hips. Sense the potential energy throughout the body. The spine and the body should feel very lifted, as if there were space between each vertebra. The top of the head should be as far away from the floor as possible. Focus forward (Illus. 1, solid lines).

ELEMENTARY

Counts 1 2 3 / 2 2 3 / 3 2 3 / 4 2 3 / 5: As though a large hand is pushing at the back of your head, fall over successively (leading with the *top* of your head) so that

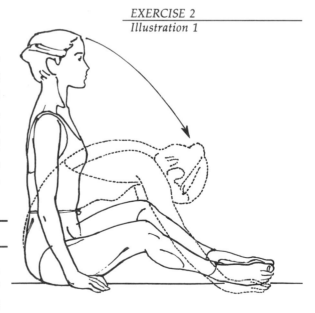

you are rounded over as far as you can go without hitting your head on your feet or the floor. The hands will slide forward along the floor toward your feet (Illus. 1, dotted lines). Allow the spine to lengthen during the fall. It is extremely important to remember to lead with the top of the head in the fall in order to avoid whipping the neck, which happens when the chin pushes forward as the head goes over. During the bounces keep the head feeling heavy, with the top of the head reaching toward the floor, so that it does not bob up and down from the neck as you bounce. Gravity determines the speed of the fall. It is the fall—the release of the potential energy and its transformation into kinetic energy—that gives you the stretch in the spine. At the bottom of the fall, the spine naturally pulls back slightly into a bounce, or rebound. Let the weight go again and bounce. As you bounce, let the momentum of each bounce and rebound build, lifting slightly on the rebound. Let momentum and gravity do the work. Keep the pelvis and hips in place; do not let them roll forward.

Counts – 2 3 / 6 2 3 / 7 2 3 / 8 2 3: On count 5 you will be at the lowest position of your fifth bounce. Use the last beats of the measure to start rising successively up to vertical, vertebra by vertebra, during counts – 2 3 / 6 2 3 / 7 2 3 / 8 2 3. As you roll up the spine, keep your focus on your navel as long as you can. The head is the heaviest part of the body and will be the last part of the body to rise.

SEQUENCE: Repeat the exercise:
4 times with the legs in the diamond shape, soles of the feet together, then
4 times with the legs straight in front, toes pointed, then
4 times with the legs apart (Illus. 2).

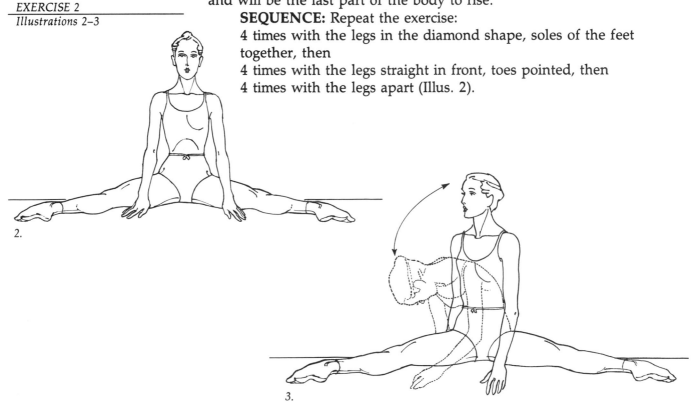

EXERCISE 2
Illustrations 2–3

2.

3.

The body always bounces over to the front in this exercise. Remember to keep the pelvis and the hips in place and think of rounding the body over. It might help you to feel the rebound if you think of your spine as an elastic that stretches out and pulls back as you bounce.

Accent the downbeat (first beat in each measure) so that the rhythm will be: *down* up up, *down* up up (like a waltz). Accenting the downbeat will help you feel the rebound.

INTERMEDIATE

Repeat the elementary sequence twice in each position. Then with the legs apart, twist the upper body at the waist so that the torso faces out over the right leg (Illus. 3, solid lines).

Counts 1 2 3 / 2 2 3 / 3 2 3 / 4 2 3 / 5: Bounce 4 times, keeping the spine rounded (Illus. 3, dotted lines). Count 5 is the rebound that starts the spine rolling up.

Counts – 2 3 / 6 2 3 / 7 2 3: On the fifth measure use the rebound to begin taking the spine successively up to vertical, keeping the upper body facing out over the right leg.

Counts 8 2 3: Use these 3 counts to change the twist of the torso to the left. You are now ready to repeat the sequence.

Repeat the sequence of 7 measures to the left, bouncing over the left leg and keeping the upper body facing out over the left leg as you roll up. On count 8, twist the torso back to the right to repeat.

SEQUENCE: Repeat the exercise:
2 times with the soles of the feet together, bouncing forward,
2 times with the legs straight in front, bouncing forward
2 times with the legs apart, bouncing forward, and
4 times with the twist in the body: right, left, right, left.

ADVANCED

Repeat the intermediate version all the way through. Return to the opening position. Repeat the entire sequence again from the beginning, at a faster tempo and with two additions: add successional arms as the body comes up to vertical, and add an arch in the upper body. The arch happens gradually as the body rolls up to vertical on counts – 2 3 / 6 2 3 / 7 2 3 / 8 2 3, so that you complete the arch by the end of 8 2 3. On the last sequence of bounces, with the legs apart and the upper body twisted, add an arch on counts 7 2 3. Maintain the arch and lift, and twist the whole body to the other side from the waist on counts 8 2 3, to begin the bounces to the next side.

The arms are added as follows: As your chest lifts, allow the lift to bring your arms across and up, hugging your sides as if you were about to pull a sweater off your head. As your spine continues to uncurl and the shoulders relax, your elbows will rise until they are overhead and your lower arms are crossed over each other. As your neck and head come to vertical, the chest will open (lift) slightly. The opening in the chest allows the shoulders to fall into place and the elbows to begin opening out to the sides. The arms continue to extend on a high diagonal from the body.

On the last sequence of bounces, with the twist, the arms remain extended on the diagonal as you arch and twist, then they relax down to your sides as you bounce.

SEQUENCE: Complete the sequence for the intermediate version. Then at an increased tempo, repeat the entire sequence as follows:

2 times with the soles of the feet together, bouncing forward, with arms and arch,

2 times with the legs in front, bouncing forward, with arms and arch,

2 times with the legs apart, bouncing forward, with arms and arch,

4 times with the twist in the body plus arms and arch: right, left, right, left.

As you arch in the chest, feel the same reach upward in your chest as you felt in the top of your head in the opening position.

The tempo can vary. It can be as fast as is comfortable without creating unnecessary tension.

Daniel Lewis teaching at the Juilliard School. PETER SCHAAF

NOTES TO TEACHERS

The most important part of this exercise is to discover how the rhythm of the bounce can take over the muscle action and can initiate and do the work. It's almost as if the body becomes a perpetual-motion machine, with a rhythm that keeps going. By using the rhythm to do the work, the muscles can stretch freely and without tension.

Labanotation for this exercise is provided on page 189.

The metronome setting for this exercise is $\dot{\bigcirc} = 63$ for elementary and intermediate levels, $\dot{\bigcirc} = 80$ for advanced.

Phrasing for musical accompaniment:

3/4 >♩♩♩ | >♩♩♩ | >♩♩♩ | >♩♩♩ | >♩. | ♩. | ♩. | ♩. ||

1 2 3 / 2 2 3 / 3 2 3 / 4 2 3 / 5 2 3 / 6 2 3 / 7 2 3 / 8 2 3

THREE: BOUNCES WITH TWIST

PURPOSE: To warm up the spine with bounces, adding a twist in the spine while successively rolling up to vertical.

I teach these bounces just as José taught them with only one minor change in the advanced version as the spine comes to vertical. José simply brought the arm up overhead. I teach students to allow the arm to come down slightly, in order to release any tension in the back, and to use the lift in the spine to bring it back overhead. I have also added the rhythmic variations at the end to help blend the oppositional pulls and the successional movements.

METER: elementary: 4/4
               intermediate and advanced: 5/4
TEMPO: medium
PHRASING: 4/4: 1 & 2 & 3 & 4 &   5/4: 1 & 2 & 3 4 5 &

OPENING POSITION: Sitting, soles of the feet together, legs in a comfortable diamond shape. The spine should be vertical and feel very long. Focus forward. (This is the same opening position as in Exercise 2, Illus. 1.)

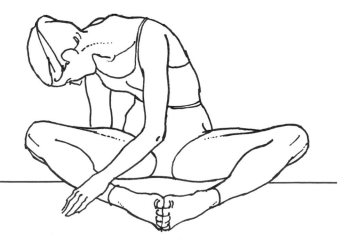

EXERCISE 3
Illustration 1

ELEMENTARY

The elementary version should be used as a preparation for all levels. In this exercise I use the & counts to help you feel the rebound rhythmically.

Counts 1 &: Drop the body over forward (head, shoulders, chest and waist) on count 1. Rebound slightly on the & count, simultaneously twisting from the waist to face over the right knee (Illus. 1).

Counts 2 &: Bounce over the right knee on count 2 and rebound on the & count, twisting the body from the waist to face to the front.

Counts 3 & 4 &: Bounce forward on count 3, rebounding to bring the spine successively up to vertical on counts & 4 &. You should feel very tall and be able to sense the potential energy in your body, ready to begin again.

Summary of Counts:

1: Bounce forward.

&: Lift and twist upper body to face out over right knee.

2: Bounce toward right knee.

&: Lift and twist upper body back to the front.

3: Bounce forward.

& 4 &: Roll spine successively up to vertical.

Use the same sequence to bounce and rebound to the left.

SEQUENCE:

Bounce forward, right, forward, roll up,

Bounce forward, left, forward, roll up.

Repeat right and left.

INTERMEDIATE

In the intermediate version the spine rolls up to vertical as you face out over the knee. Do the elementary version first in order to prepare the body and build the energy so that you can go directly into the intermediate version. Both the intermediate version and the advanced version are in 5 counts.

Counts 1 &: Drop the body over forward (head, shoulders, chest and waist) on count 1. Rebound on the & count, simultaneously twisting from the waist to face over the right knee (Illus. 2, solid lines).

Counts 2 &: Bounce over the right knee on count 2 and rebound on the & count.

Counts 3 & 4 &: Maintaining the twist in the upper body over the right knee, use the rebound on the & count of 2 to begin to roll succession-

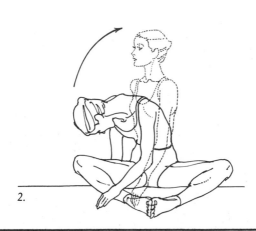

EXERCISE 3
Illustrations 2–3

2.

3.

ally up to vertical (Illus. 2, dotted lines). As you roll up, keep your focus on your navel as long you can. Your shoulders and head should finish facing directly to the right side.

Counts 5 &: Twist the body to face front, making sure to keep the spine and head lifted. Feel the lift coming from the high point at the top of the head. Your gaze should be forward. Be careful not to lift from the chin.

SEQUENCE:
Once through the elementary version: right, left, right, left (in 4/4).
Then in 5/4:
Bounce forward, right, roll up, face forward,
Bounce forward, left, roll up, face forward.
Repeat right and left.

ADVANCED

In the advanced version a side bend with an arm movement is added. Begin by doing the entire elementary exercise, then go directly into the intermediate sequence. As you finish each 5 count, lift the arm on the & count of 5 and curve it overhead (Illus. 3).

Counts 1 &: Fall to the right (head, shoulders, chest and waist) into a side bend. The right hand can be placed on the floor as you fall, palm down. The high point on the left side of the ribcage should be lifting up (Illus. 4). Feel the opposition between the head, as it reaches down toward the floor to the right, and the left hip, as it reaches down toward the floor to the left. The left hip can come up off the floor slightly.

Counts 2 &: Rotate the left shoulder and extend the left arm sequentially—elbow, arm, hand, palm facing out—to the right (Illus. 5, solid lines). Simultaneously twist the upper body so that the chest and shoulders are parallel to the floor. The focus is down. As you twist if you think of lifting the right shoulder and lowering the left shoulder, it will help you to get your chest parallel to the floor.

EXERCISE 3
Illustrations 4–6

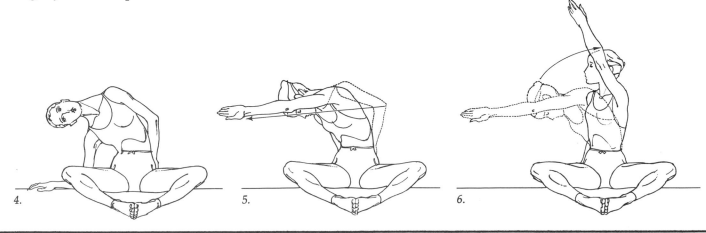

4.   5.   6.

Counts 3 & 4 & 5: Beginning at the base of the spine, start to roll the spine successively up to vertical, lowering the arm slightly, and allowing the arm to rotate so the palm faces in. As the middle of the back (thoracic) begins to come up, the arm lifts along with it, until the body is vertical, facing right, and the arm is overhead. The body and arm should arrive on count 5 (Illus. 6).

Count & of 5: Return the body to face front, keeping the arm curved overhead, ready to begin on the left.

SEQUENCE:
Once through elementary version: right, left, right, left (in 4/4).
Once through intermediate version: right, left, right, left (in 5/4).
Fall right, extend left arm, roll up, face forward.
Fall left, extend right arm, roll up, face forward.
Repeat right and left.

As you do the side bend, keep the focus forward. Make sure that you feel the vertical stretch (the high point) in each part of the exercise. Feel all the oppositional pulls in the body. For example, as the arm extends to the side try to sense the diagonal pull between the tips of fingers and the lower spine (lumbar). Maintain that feeling of stretch as the arm lowers slightly and then lifts above the head in the roll up.

ADVANCED VARIATIONS

The following variations introduce rhythmic changes and should be accomplished one right after the other, without stopping. Try to blend all the movements together into a steady flow, without stops or starts. The only time you stop briefly is just before count 1 as you come to vertical, when you suspend the movement for just a moment before continuing. These changes in phrasing and the rhythm of the movement help to create the style.

FIRST VARIATION: Change the exercise from a 5-count phrase to a 3-count phrase by making each action happen on 1 count. The tempo remains the same, but the meter changes to 3/4.

Count 1: Fall into side bend.
Count 2: Shoulder rotates and arm extends.
Count 3: Body and arm successively lift to vertical.
Count & of 3: Return to face front.
Repeat 2 to 4 times.

SECOND VARIATION: Change the exercise from a 3-count phrase to a 2-count phrase (2/4 meter). The accent is on the & count and the tempo remains the same.

Count 1: Fall into side bend.

Count & of 1: Shoulder rotates and arm extends.

Count 2: Body and arm successively lift to vertical.

Count & of 2: Return to face forward.

THIRD VARIATION: Change the exercise to a 1-count phrase. Eliminate the accents and blend all the movements together. You may want to slow the tempo slightly.

Count 1: Fall into side bend, rotate shoulder and extend arm, bring body and arm successively up to vertical.

Count & of 1: Return to face forward.

NOTES TO TEACHERS

I always use the 4-count elementary version as a preparation for the intermediate and advanced versions in order to set up the rhythm in the body.

When doing the variations, try to have the students accomplish the exercise as one continuous movement. In other words, the shoulder begins to rotate before the side bend is completed, the impetus in the spine to begin the successional rise comes before the arm has finished moving, and so forth. All movements still must be executed fully, however. The two movements that often get muddied as the exercise speeds up are the extension of the arm and the completion of the successional rise. Stress the moment at the end of the exercise when the spine is lengthened and the body contains the most potential energy, just before the fall into the next side bend.

Labanotation for this exercise is provided on page 191.

The metronome setting for this exercise is ♩ = 44.

Phrasing for musical accompaniment:

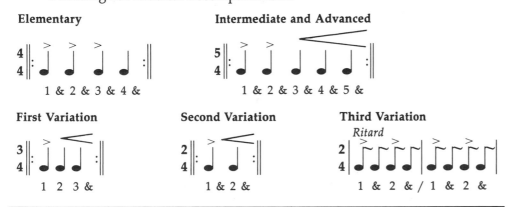

Elementary

4/4 ‖: > > > :‖
1 & 2 & 3 & 4 &

Intermediate and Advanced

5/4 ‖: > > :‖
1 & 2 & 3 & 4 & 5 &

First Variation

3/4 ‖: > :‖
1 2 3 &

Second Variation

2/4 ‖: > :‖
1 & 2 &

Third Variation

Ritard

2/4 | > > > > |
1 & 2 & / 1 & 2 &

Center Exercises

FOUR: STANDING BOUNCES

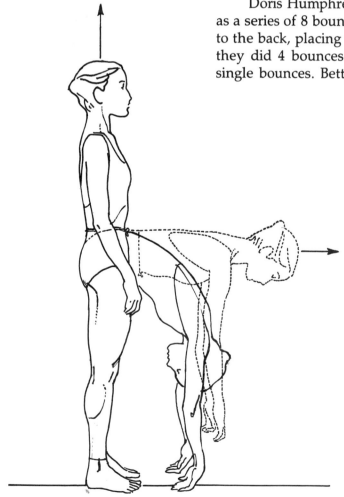

PURPOSE: To release the muscles around the back and spine, allowing the ribcage to drop down and relax.

Doris Humphrey, Charles Weidman and José Limón did this exercise as a series of 8 bounces forward, 8 to the right side, 8 to the left and then 8 to the back, placing the hands on the hips to hold the pelvis in place; then they did 4 bounces in each direction, 2 in each direction, and 4 sets of single bounces. Betty Jones broke the bounces down by isolating the tilt, the rounding over, and the hissing to release the muscles of the spine. She also took out the bounces to the back, which can be hard on the lumbar vertebrae.

METER: 4/4
TEMPO: medium
PHRASING: elementary:

1 2 3 4 / 2 2 3 4 / 3 2 3 4 / 1 2 3 4 / 5 6 7 8
intermediate and advanced:

1 2 3 4 / 2 2 3 4 / 1 2 3 4 / 5 6 7 8

OPENING POSITION: Standing, legs parallel, feet directly below hips, spine straight and long. Feel the lift coming from the top of the head. The weight should be evenly distributed on both feet and evenly distributed between the toes and the heels (Illus. 1, upright figure).

PREPARATION (ALL LEVELS): Now, in order to center properly while standing, take a deep breath. Think of filling your head with helium and begin to rise from the top of the head until your heels lift off the floor and you are in a high relevé.

Try to feel as if the helium in your head is lifting your body so high that your legs just hang from your hips, rather than as if you were pushing up into relevé from the feet. Let the breath out slowly, hissing as you exhale, and slowly lower the heels back to the floor. Repeat the relevé, breathing normally, and try to create the same sensation of filling with air. As you lower your heels, think of leaving the head where it is, very lifted, and allowing the heels to stretch toward the floor, lengthening the calves, thighs and spine. You should feel very tall.

ELEMENTARY

Counts 1 2 3 4: Bend forward from the hip joints, keeping the back flat, until the back is parallel to the floor—at a 90-degree angle to the legs like a tabletop (Illus. 1, dotted lines). As you do this, try to keep your hips over your feet rather than allowing them to move back.

Counts 2 2 3 4: Beginning with the top of the head, take the head over toward the floor, and allow the weight of the head to pull the spine over, vertebra by vertebra (Illus. 1). Relax the spine at the bottom of the stretch.

Counts 3 2 3 4: Take a deep breath, allowing the ribcage to expand as much as possible, exhale and hiss for all 4 counts. Feel the muscles around the spine and ribcage release.

Counts 1 2 3 4: Bounce 4 times, once on each count. Allow the bounces to build and get slightly higher with each rebound.

Counts 5 6 7 8: Bounce once more on count 5 and use the rebound of this bounce to begin the successional rise of the spine, vertebra by vertebra, back up to vertical, on counts 6 7 and 8. By count 8 you should reach vertical and feel as tall and lifted as you did in the opening position.

This bounce and unrolling of the spine contains all the elements of successional flow in the spine (see page 188).

Repeat to the right:
Counts 1 2 3 4: Begin in the opening position (Illus. 2, solid lines). Instead of tilting forward with a flat back, this time tilt the whole spine and head in one piece toward the right, keeping the back as long and straight as possible (Illus. 2, first dotted figure). The legs and hips remain stationary.

Counts 2 2 3 4: Beginning with the top of the head, take the head down to the right, allowing the weight of the

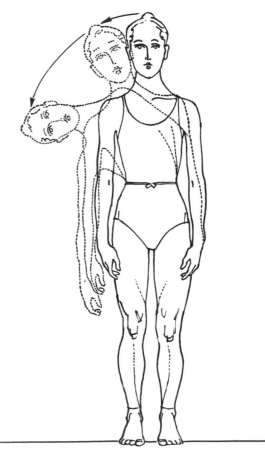

EXERCISE 4
Illustration 2

head to pull the spine over, vertebra by vertebra, into a side bend to the right. Keep your focus front. Imagine your body arching over the top of a barrel, so that your waist remains lifted (Illus. 2, second dotted figure).

Counts 3 2 3 4: Take a deep breath and exhale, hissing, for 4 counts. This will help lengthen the spine and relax the ribcage.

Counts 1 2 3 4: Bounce to the right 4 times, once on each count, lifting slightly higher with each rebound.

Counts 5 6 7 8: Bounce once more on count 5 and allow the rebound to begin to bring the spine, vertebra by vertebra, back up to vertical. Once again feel very tall. After you have finished the exercise, go right into a relevé to check your alignment.

SEQUENCE: 2 times: forward, right, left

If you are having trouble feeling the rhythm and the build of the bounce, try subdividing each bounce count into three beats: $\overset{>}{1}$ 2 3 / $\overset{>}{2}$ 2 3 / $\overset{>}{3}$ 2 3, and so forth. Bounce on the downbeat and use the 2 3 to rebound and lift. Then go back and do the exercise with one bounce to each count.

The rhythm of the movement creates the phrasing and helps to emphasize the quality. Once you get the rhythm of the bounces in your body, the rhythm will take over and less muscle action will be required to do the movement. As tension is released from the muscles, the contrast of the heavy quality of the bounce on the downbeat and the lighter quality of the lift in the body becomes clearer.

INTERMEDIATE

Do the elementary version once through, then go immediately into the intermediate version, which is the same as the elementary with the addition of successional arms (Illus. 5, page 40) and the elimination of the breathing in and hissing out.

Counts 1 2 3 4: Tilt forward.

Counts 2 2 3 4: Take the head and spine successionally over forward.

Counts 1 2 3 4: Bounce 4 times, once on each count.

Counts 5 6 7 8: Bounce once on count 5 and use the rebound to bring the spine successionally back up to vertical. As the spine rises, bring the arms up successionally. The elbows should be overhead by count 7. Open them out to the sides on count 8.

Repeat to the right adding the left arm just after the rebound on count 5. The arm uncurls successionally overhead and out to the left side as the spine comes back up to vertical. Repeat to the left, using the right arm.

Do the entire exercise all the way through twice. After you have finished the exercise, go directly into a relevé to check your alignment.

SEQUENCE:
Once through the elementary version, then
2 times: forward, right, left.

ADVANCED

Do the elementary version once through, the intermediate version once through, and go directly into the advanced version, which is identical to the intermediate but at a fast tempo. As you do the exercise in the fast tempo, really try to use the weight of the body in the rebound to do all the work of lifting. After you have finished the exercise, ending with the right arm overhead, take a relevé and simultaneously lower the arm down to the side. Feel the connection between the hand as it lowers and the top of the head as it rises.

SEQUENCE:
Once through the elementary version,
Once through the intermediate version, then
Twice through the advanced version (fast tempo).

NOTES TO TEACHERS

This exercise is working on standing alignment. Watch that the weight stays evenly placed between the legs and is evenly distributed between the toes and heels. This will ensure a stable base. Students often throw all their weight into their toes as they take the forward or side bend.

Labanotation for this exercise is provided on page 192.

The metronome setting for this exercise is ♩ = 69 for the elementary and intermediate levels, ♩ = 92 for the advanced.

Phrasing for musical accompaniment:

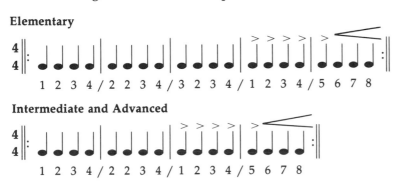

Elementary

1 2 3 4 / 2 2 3 4 / 3 2 3 4 / 1 2 3 4 / 5 6 7 8

Intermediate and Advanced

1 2 3 4 / 2 2 3 4 / 1 2 3 4 / 5 6 7 8

FIVE: TENDU SERIES

PURPOSE: To warm up the ankles and the feet, while maintaining your center. The knee and hip joints are warmed up in this exercise as well.

José always taught tendus at the barre, with different degrees and variations of body bend. I teach tendus in the center in order to work on centering the body without the aid of the barre and on keeping the hips properly placed. This builds a kinetic sense of placement that is important later when going across the floor.

METER: 3/4
TEMPO: slow, then fast

PHRASING: 1 2 3 / 2 2 3 / 3 2 3 4 5 6

OPENING POSITION: Standing in first position, arms relaxed, down by your sides. Take the right leg out to the side, brushing the foot along the floor and keeping the toes pointed (Illus. 1). Concentrate on lifting in the upper body and on keeping the hips aligned just as if you were standing on both feet.

EXERCISE 5
Illustration 1

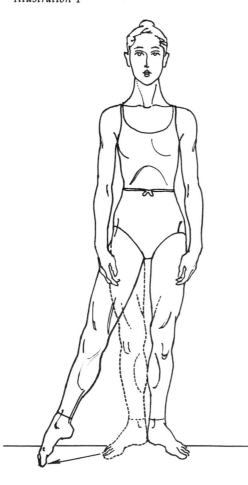

ELEMENTARY

Counts 1 2 3: Close into first position, brushing the foot along the floor, then brush the foot back out to the side into the opening position. The action should be even and smooth, with no accent as the heels come together. Use all 3 counts to accomplish this; try to avoid closing sharply on 1 and brushing out on 2 3.

Counts 2 2 3: Repeat the first 3 counts, closing into first position and brushing the foot back out to the side.

Counts 3 2 3 4 5 6: Close into first position and plié on counts 3 2 3. On counts 4 5 6, lift in the torso to straighten the legs and simultaneously release the left leg to the side, brushing the foot along the floor. The left leg should be stretched, toes pointed, ready to begin the brushes with the left foot.

Repeat the tendus to the left, right, and left.

Then do the exercise another 4 times, right, left, right, left, adding the body as follows:

Counts 1 2 3 / 2 2 3: Same as above.

Counts 3 2 3: As you bring the right leg in to first position and plié, take the body over forward (Illus. 2, dotted lines). The arms stay relaxed.

Counts 4 5 6: Uncurl the spine successionally as you lift to straighten the legs and as the left foot brushes out to the side. The body should reach vertical by count 6.

Then repeat the sequence to the left, right, and left, adding the forward body drop and successional roll up with each plié.

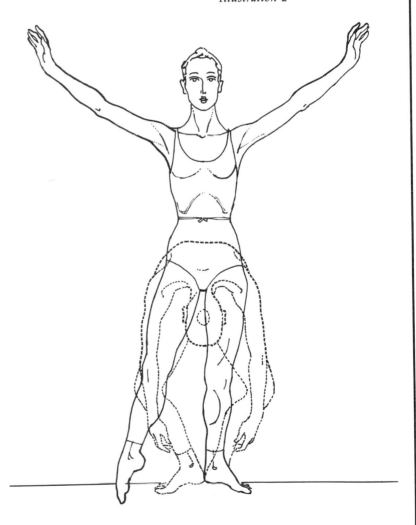

EXERCISE 5
Illustration 2

Repeat the sequence 4 more times, right, left, right, left, adding arms as follows: The arms stay down on 1 2 3 / 2; they lift out successionally to the sides on counts – 2 3 (Illus. 2, solid lines). The arms drop as the body falls on counts 3 2 3 and then successionally rise and open to the sides as the spine rolls up on counts 4 5 6. Allow the arms to drop quickly to your sides on the next count 1. The palms of your hands will hit the sides of your legs.

At this point there is a 4-count transition: in 4 counts, brush the right foot back into first position, plié, and tendu the left foot to the side. You are now ready to repeat the entire sequence, this time beginning to the left, and at a quicker tempo. The fast tempo will cause the drop in the body to become a rebound and will therefore change the count as follows:

Counts 1 2 3 / 2 2 3: Same as above (at the fast tempo).

Count 3: Brush the right foot in, plié and drop the body over forward and rebound. (Imagine a hand pushing the back of your head over.)

Counts – 2 3 4 5 6: Use the rebound to

bring the spine back up to vertical. The lift in the spine allows the legs to straighten and causes the arms to rise successively and open to the sides.

SEQUENCE:
At the slow tempo:
Repeat 4 simple tendus: right, left, right, left,
4 tendus with body: right, left, right, left,
4 tendus with body and arms: right, left, right, left,
4-count transition.
Repeat entire sequence at fast tempo, starting with left foot.

Daniel Lewis teaching tendus at the Juilliard School.

PETER SCHAAF

Accomplish the curling and uncurling of the spine as smoothly and comfortably as possible. Keep in mind that it is the lift in the body that allows the legs to straighten underneath you, rather than the legs pushing upward.

INTERMEDIATE

The intermediate version is the same as the elementary, with the addition of half turns. Do the 4 simple tendus first without adding the body, then do the tendus with half turns as described below, then add the body, and finally add the arms.

Counts 1 2 3 / 2 2 3: Same as simple tendus. Start the tendus with the right foot.

Counts 3 2 3 4 5 6: Here is where the turns are added. Instead of closing into first, close the right foot in front into an open fifth position (about three inches between the feet), plié, and turn a half turn (180-degree) counterclockwise, staying in plié and using the turn-out in the legs to accomplish the turn. Lift to straighten the legs on counts 4 5 6 and simultaneously extend the left leg out to the side to begin to the left. Keep your weight lifted and centered.

Repeat this 4 times, right, left, right, left. When you tendu with the left foot, the half turn will go clockwise.

Then add the body and do the tendus with half turns and the body. Drop the body over on the count of 3, and turn as you come up to vertical on – 2 3 4 5 6. Repeat this 4 times.

Then add the arms and do the tendus with half turns, arms and body. Repeat this 4 times.

SEQUENCE:
Repeat at the slow tempo:
4 simple tendus: right, left, right, left,
4 tendus with half turns: right, left, right, left,
4 tendus with half turns and body: right, left, right, left,
4 tendus with half turns, body and arms: right, left, right, left,
4-count transition.
Repeat entire sequence at fast tempo, starting with left foot.

As you add the body, it becomes very important to maintain the center axis and to use the rebound to take the weight out of the legs as you rise, in order to accomplish the turn. The timing of the body is very important: if you come up too fast or too slowly, it will throw your turn off. Take the full 5 counts to complete the rise in the body. At the fast tempo, use the rebound to help you lift.

ADVANCED

The advanced version is the same as the intermediate, with the substitution of full turns for half turns.

SEQUENCE:
Repeat at the slow tempo:
4 simple tendus: right, left, right, left,
4 tendus with full turns: right, left, right, left,
4 tendus with full turns and body: right, left, right, left,
4 tendus with full turns, body and arms: right, left, right, left,
4-count transition.
Repeat entire sequence at fast tempo, starting with left foot.

ADVANCED VARIATION

Do the tendus 4 times with full turns and successional arms, adding the body and a passé as follows: Drop into a side bend (toward the working leg) as you plié on count 3. Swing the body forward on the 2 of count 3 and rebound as you go into the full turn and bring the spine up to vertical. As you turn, the weight will transfer onto the working leg. Bring the other leg into passé. Be sure to keep the body moving from the side bend into the forward drop and rebound. This will help you come up on center on counts 3 4 5 6 into a full passé. Make sure you feel the opposition in the arms; this will help you to balance.

It is the timing and rhythm of the body as it swings, drops forward and rebounds that keeps the momentum going. If you keep both hips aligned underneath you, maintain the lift from the high point and try not to push from your feet, you will not be thrown off balance. This is a very hard exercise and should be attempted only by professional dancers.

NOTES TO TEACHERS

The rhythm of the rebound controls the successional rise of the spine and the turns. I find it quite helpful for the students if I sing the rhythm, or musical phrasing, to them as they do the exercise. I often have the dancers themselves sing or make sounds as they are doing the exercise in order for them to really feel how the rhythm in the body meets the musical phrasing.

When the student begins to add turns, before adding the body be sure that the weight is centered evenly between both legs during the turn. If the weight is uneven during the turn, the balance will be thrown off when the body is added.

Labanotation for this exercise is provided on page 193.

The metronome setting for this exercise is $\quad$ = 50 for the elementary level and $\quad$ = 80 for the intermediate and advanced.

Phrasing for musical accompaniment:

1 2 3 / 2 2 3 / 3 2 3 / 4 5 6

SIX: PLIÉ SERIES

PURPOSE: To warm up the thighs, calves and ankles, and to practice using fall and recovery in the body to take you into relevé.

José always taught pliés at the barre with the body going over immediately and an exhale as the legs plié. He also taught them with the body vertical on the plié, going over at the bottom of the plié and coming up successively as the legs straighten. We would face the barre and take the pliés in first, second, right foot front in fifth, and left foot front in fifth; then in all positions with one arm on the barre, taking the body over to the right; then in all positions taking the body over the left. I have taken the pliés away from the barre and connected the fall and rise in the body in order to keep the movement from stopping at the bottom of the plié. I have also eliminated the exhaling on the pliés.

METER: 2/2
TEMPO: between slow and medium

PHRASING: 1 2 / 3 4 / 5 6

OPENING POSITION: Standing in first position, arms down at the sides.

PREPARATION (ALL LEVELS): Starting with the lift in the high point at the top of the head, take five counts to lift into a relevé. The legs should feel long and released, as if they were hanging from the hips. On the sixth count bring the heels down to the floor and try to leave the top of the head lifted so that the whole spine feels stretched. Imagine a string attached to the top of your head that keeps pulling up as you lower the heels. Go directly from this preparation into the exercise.

EXERCISE 6
Illustration 1

ELEMENTARY

Counts 1 2: Grand plié (Illus. 1).

Counts 3 4 5 6: Drop the body (head, shoulders, chest and waist) over forward, leading with the top of the head (Illus. 2, solid lines). At the same time the heels go to the floor, and the hips rise automatically. Use the energy of the hips rising to straighten the legs and begin the spine uncurling. By count 4, the legs should be straight, the upper body (head, shoulders, chest and a part of the waist) still slightly curved (Illus. 2, dotted lines). On counts 4 5, lift in the body to bring the spine to vertical and simultaneously lift into a relevé (Illus. 3). Lower the heels on count 6. As in the preparation, feel the string pulling the top of the head up as the heels

EXERCISE 6
Illustrations 2–3

2.

3.

lower. Go right into another plié without stopping. Each time you lift into the relevé, be sure that it is the lift that creates the relevé, rather than a push upward from the feet. The movement should be smooth and continuous.

Repeat, taking the body bend to the right: initiate the side bend with the top of the head. As the heels come down from the grand plié, the top of the head goes farther toward the floor. As the hips rise and the legs begin to straighten bring the body up successionally. Be sure to keep the high point traveling up the side of the ribcage as you come up to vertical and into relevé. Repeat, taking the body bend to the left.

Do the entire exercise (forward, right, left) all the way through twice.

SEQUENCE:
Grand plié, body forward,
Grand plié, body to the right,
Grand plié, body to the left.
Repeat the entire sequence.

This is the same fall in the body that you use in the bounces. The difference here is that instead of using the momentum of the fall to create a rebound to bounce the body back up to vertical, you transfer that energy and momentum into the heels as the head drops toward the floor and allow it to travel up through the body and spine.

INTERMEDIATE

Do the elementary version all the way through once. The second time through, add successional arms, beginning on count 4 and continuing through the end of the exercise. The arms are exactly the same as in Exercise Four.

SEQUENCE:
Once through the elementary version, then
Grand plié, body forward, with arms,
Grand plié, body to the right, with left arm,
Grand plié, body to the left, with right arm.

ADVANCED

This version takes the body off center; the upper body works *around* the vertical axis. Do the elementary version all the way through once. The next time through, do the arms (intermediate version) and add the body as follows (the & counts have been added to help you find the positions).

Counts 1 & 2 &: Grand plié.

Count 3: Drop the body over forward and bring the heels down to the floor.

Count &: Take the body to the right in a side bend, as the hips begin to rise.

Counts 4 &: Take the upper body into an arch as the hips continue to rise and the legs straighten. The top of your head will describe a quarter circle as the left arm rises successively, crossing the body, and curves overhead.

Counts 5 & 6 &: Lift into relevé as the chest comes back to vertical and the arm opens out to the left. On the count of 6 &, lower the heels and bring the arm down to the side.

Repeat, with the side bend to the left.

SEQUENCE:
Once through the elementary version, then
once through the intermediate version, then
Grand plié, body to the right, through the arch and to the vertical, with the left arm,
Grand plié, body to the left, through the arch and to the vertical, with the right arm.
Repeat right and left.

NOTES TO TEACHERS

The advanced version can be done without the arms if the student is having difficulty with the movement in the body.

If the student is having trouble connecting the body lift to the relevé, have him or her practice just counts 5 and 6 in order to find how the high point in the spine takes the body into relevé. This can also be practiced at the barre.

Labanotation for the preparation, intermediate and advanced versions of this exercise is provided on page 194.

The metronome setting for this exercise is $\bullet$ = 44.

Phrasing for musical accompaniment:

1 2 / 3 4 / 5 6

SEVEN: SWINGS IN SECOND

PURPOSE: To isolate the head, shoulders, chest, waist and hips in a swing movement and to create moments of suspension in the side bends.

There is no difference between the way I teach this exercise and the way Doris Humphrey, Charles Weidman and José Limón taught it, though José did occasionally add variations. To the hip swings, he added a body twist and roll up on the diagonal. I added some full turns to the hip swings, but only for my very advanced students. Neither variation is included here.

METER: 3/4
TEMPO: very slow

PHRASING: 1 2 3 / 2 2 3 / 3 2 3 4 5 6

OPENING POSITION: Standing with feet in a wide second position; head is tilted to the right, focus front. Feel the lift in the high point in the neck. The arms are down at the sides.

ALL LEVELS

In each set of swings you will make a half circle, another half circle, then a circle and a half.

Counts 1 2 3: Swing the head forward and to the left, making a half circle and ending with the head tilted to the left, focus front (Illus. 1). On count 3, feel the lift in the high point in the neck and suspend the lift. In other words, try to keep the lift from the high point continuing until the very last moment before you drop your head to begin the swings to the right.

Counts 2 2 3: Reverse the head swing, making a half circle that goes from left to right. Feel the high point in the neck and suspend the lift on count 3.

Counts 3 2 3 4 5 6: Swing head forward, left, back, right, then forward again and left (a circle and a half), so that you end with the head tilted to the left, focus front. Try to sense the high point in the neck during the swings. Suspend the lift briefly as the head goes to the back and more fully as the head goes to the side on count 6.

Repeat, starting the head swings toward the right.

Repeat the head swings, adding the shoulders. The high point will now be at the base of the neck. As the head swings forward, let the shoulders fall forward and then let them open as the head swings to the left (Illus. 2). In the circle-and-a-half swing, as the head swings to the back, allow the shoulders to open more fully. The shoulder blades will pull together in the back. Keep the head swinging freely as you add the shoulders. Each time you swing to the side, be sure to keep the focus front and keep both shoulders square to the front. Throughout the swing maintain the lift in the high point and suspend on the counts of 3 and on count 6.

Repeat, beginning the swing toward the right.

Now add the chest to the head and shoulder swings (Illus. 3). The high point will now be in the upper back, right between the shoulder blades. Keep the swing of the head and the shoulders going as you add the chest. Each time you swing to the side, be sure to keep the focus front and the shoulders square to the front. As the chest swings around to the back, allow the upper body to arch. Continue to lift from the high point and suspend the swing.

Repeat, beginning the swing toward the right.

EXERCISE 7
Illustrations 1–3

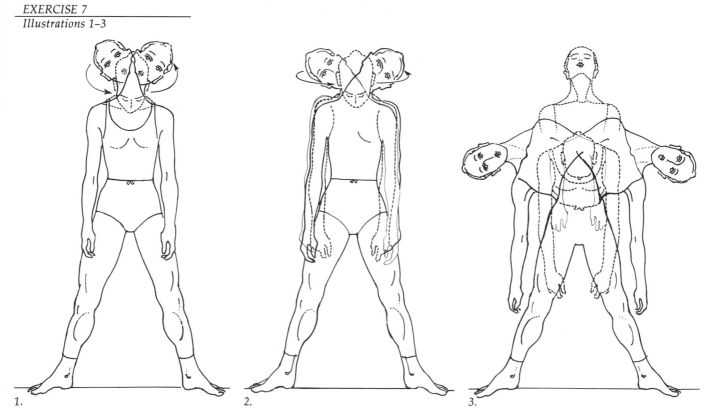

1.   2.   3.

This time add the waist (Illus. 4), and keep the head, shoulders and chest swinging. The high point will travel to the lower back (the lumbar). Each time you swing to the side, focus front and keep the shoulders and chest square to the front. As the body swings around to the back, only the upper body (head, shoulders, chest) should arch. Be sure not to take the arch in the lower back and not to push the hips forward.

Repeat, beginning the swing toward the right.

Repeat the exercise one last time, adding the hips (Illus. 5). The high point will be at the base of the spine as the body swings forward, and in the lower ribcage as the body swings to the side. As the body swings forward, the hips will move back to compensate. As the body swings to the side, the hips should come back underneath you, rather than push out to the opposite side. You will be in a deep side bend in which the head is over as far toward the floor as it can go, focus is front, and there is a lift and stretch in the lower ribcage. As the body swings to the back, the hips should remain underneath you. Again, be sure to arch in the upper back only.

Repeat, beginning the swing toward the right.

EXERCISE 7
Illustrations 4–5

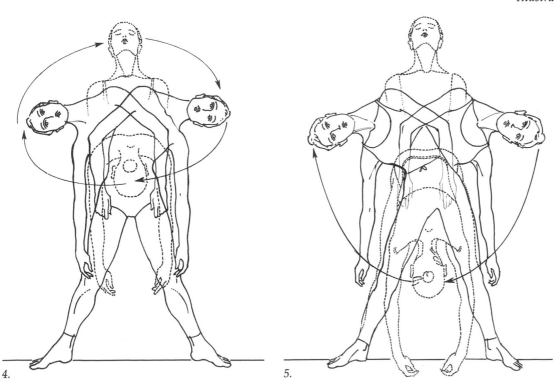

4.

5.

SEQUENCE:

2 sets of head swings: one toward the left, one toward the right,

2 sets of head and shoulder swings: one toward the left, one toward the right,

2 sets of head, shoulder and chest swings: one toward the left, one toward the right,

2 sets of head, shoulder, chest and waist swings: one toward the left, one toward the right,

2 sets of head, shoulder, chest, waist and hip swings: one toward the left, one toward the right.

All these swings should have the weighted quality of a pendulum swing: drop, swing, suspend; drop, swing, suspend.

Be sure to maintain the lift in the high point throughout the swing. As you add parts of the body the high point will travel down the spine.

Each time you take the swing to the side, suspend the side bend on the end of each phrase before continuing the swing. The top of your head will keep reaching toward the floor as the high point lifts in the suspension.

NOTES TO TEACHERS

Check that the path of the head in the swings makes a rounded C, or semicircular, shape, not a V shape. The C-shaped path causes two pulls to occur in opposition as the head swings from forward to the side—the pull of the top of the head toward the floor and the pull of the high point reaching upward.

Speed is not important in this exercise. The swings can be accomplished as slowly as needed for the students to feel the full range of movement without losing the sense of fall, as the body drops, and recovery, which takes the body into the side suspension.

Labanotation for this exercise is provided on page 195.

The metronome setting for this exercise is ♩ = 80.

Phrasing for musical accompaniment:

1 2 3 / 2 2 3 / 3 2 3 / 4 5 6

EIGHT: REBOUNDS IN THREES

PURPOSE: To connect rebound in the knees to rebound in the spine.

The elementary and intermediate versions of this exercise appear here just as José taught them. In the advanced version I have added a turn so that students can work on the timing of the body as it makes a circle around the turn of the hips, and also work on how the speed of the body turning relates to the speed of the hips turning.

EXERCISE 8
Illustration 1

METER: 3/4
TEMPO: elementary: slow   intermediate and advanced: medium

PHRASING: elementary: 1̇ 2 3/ 2̇ 2 3/ 3̇ 2 3 4 5 6

intermediate and advanced: 1̇ 2 3/ 2̇ 2 3/ 3̇ 2 3/ 4 2 3/ 5 2 3

OPENING POSITION: Standing, legs parallel, focus forward. Arms are down at the sides.

PREPARATION (ALL LEVELS): Starting in the opening position, bend your knees and curve your head, shoulders and chest over forward. Have someone place a hand on your back between your shoulder blades and gently push, as if bouncing a ball. Your shoulders should be aligned over your hips, weight evenly distributed between both feet. Your body should feel relaxed and your knees loose.

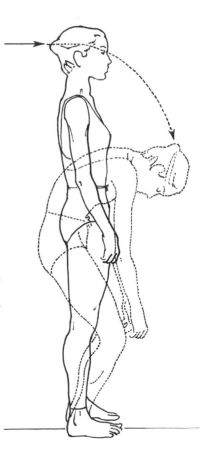

ELEMENTARY

Count 1: Drop your upper body over forward from the back of your head (exactly as in the bounces in Exercise Two), arms relaxed, and feel the rebound. Allow the knees to bend and rebound simultaneously with the spine (Illus. 1).

Counts – 2 3: From the rebound in the upper body successionally roll the spine back up to vertical. It is the lift in the body that will allow the legs to straighten. Use both counts: you should reach vertical, feeling very tall and lengthened in the spine, by count 3.

Count 2: Drop the upper body into a side bend to the right, from the top of the head, and feel the rebound. Allow the knees to bend and rebound as the spine rebounds (Illus. 2).

Counts – 2 3: Use both counts to rebound and successively roll the spine back to vertical, allowing the lift in the body to straighten the legs.

Count 3: Repeat the fall and rebound to the left.

Counts – 2 3: This time, as the spine rolls up to vertical, let the lift in the body straighten the legs and continue the lift into relevé. Imagine a pulley system working in your body: as the spine rolls back to vertical and you lift into relevé, the right side goes down and the left side goes up. Suspend the relevé.

Counts 4 5 6: Slowly lower the heels to the floor. Think of the top of the head lifting to the ceiling as the heels come down.

SEQUENCE:

Rebound forward, right, left, relevé, then
Rebound forward, left, right, relevé;
Repeat once through.

EXERCISE 8
Illustrations 2–3

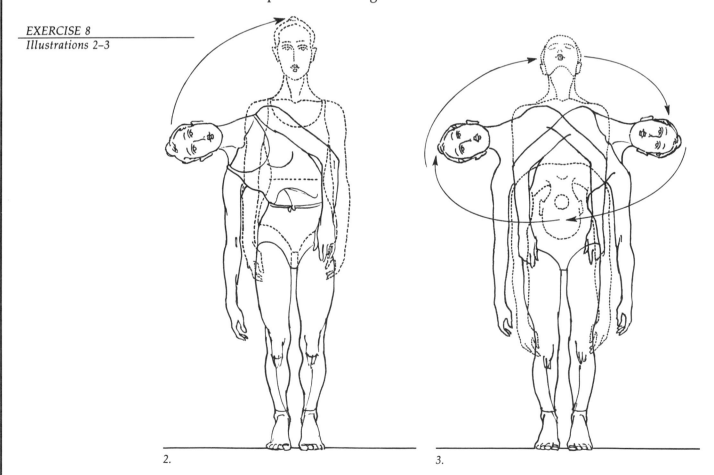

2.   3.

In all versions, it is the lift in the spine that straightens the legs. Reach the peak of the movement each time you come to vertical, lifting as tall as you can before beginning the next drop.

INTERMEDIATE

In the intermediate and advanced versions the phrasing changes to 5 measures of 3 beats each.

Counts 1 2 3/ 2 2 3/ 3 2 3: Same as elementary.

Counts 4 2 3: From the relevé, fall to the right side, bending the knees as your heels meet the floor. Swing the body forward, left and back, arching in the upper body only (exactly as in the head, shoulders, chest and waist swing in Exercise Seven). The legs stay in plié and the pelvis does not move (Illus. 3).

Counts 5 2 3: Keep the swing going and fall to the right and forward on count 5, rebounding to come up to vertical on counts 2 3.

Repeat, beginning with the body dropping forward, then to the left and to the right. Take the upper body swing on counts 4 2 3 beginning toward the left.

SEQUENCE:
Rebound forward, right, left, then
body swing toward the right;
Rebound forward, left, right, then
body swing toward the left.
Repeat once through.

Keep lifting in the high point during the body swing. This will keep the weight out of your legs and hips and will help to keep the movement smooth and easy.

ADVANCED

The advanced version is identical to the intermediate version, with the addition of a full turn on counts 4 2 3.

Counts 4 2 3/5: From the relevé, fall toward the right side on count 4, bending the knees. As the body swings forward and to the left, use the momentum of the swing to turn the body a half turn counterclockwise, pivoting on the left foot. Let the right foot skim the floor as you turn. Keep the swing in the body going into an arch to the back and to your right, which will keep the turn going and take you back around to the front. In other words, do the body swing exactly as you did in the intermediate version. Complete a half turn as the body swings toward your left side and complete another half turn through count 5 as the body swings toward your right.

Counts – 2 3: Finish the turn, keeping the body swing going from the right side over forward. Rebound and roll up to vertical.

SEQUENCE:
Rebound forward, right, left, then
body drops right, swing and turn toward the left;
Rebound forward, left, right, then
body drops left, swing and turn toward the right.
Repeat once through.

In the advanced version, keep lifting the high point so the movement is light and smooth, and use the momentum of the body swing to make the turn.

NOTES TO TEACHERS

In the elementary version, be sure students are using the body to lift into relevé. You can have them practice just that part of the exercise. This will be particularly important when they get to the intermediate and advanced versions, as pushing from the ankles will throw the body off balance.

Be sure advanced students master the coordination of the body swing and turn before attempting it in Exercise Nine.

Labanotation for this exercise is provided on page 196.

The metronome setting for this exercise is ♩ = 92 for the elementary level and ♩ = 104 for intermediate and advanced.

Phrasing for musical accompaniment:

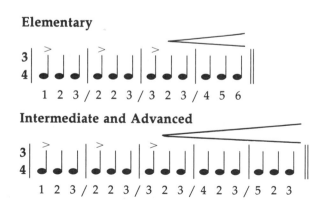

NINE: SLOW TWOS, FAST THREES

PURPOSE: To feel equal opposition between all five extremities—head, hands and feet—as they extend into space. Each extremity has four possible pairings, or oppositions (head with right hand, head with left hand, head with right foot, head with left foot, right hand with right foot, right hand with left foot, and so forth).

This exercise combines one that we did with José at the barre with the body bends in the Preparatory Exercise #2 for Fall and Rebound in the Legs that appears in Part Two. When we did this exercise with José, we did only the "fast threes" version, with both feet on the floor. We took the body bends forward, to the sides, and back with the pliés, but returned to vertical rather than reverse the body bends, as I have done here. I have added the "slow twos" part of the exercise in order to center the weight between both feet and to work on getting a smooth and even quality to the movement. All other variations and developments on the exercise that appear here are also my own.

METER: slow twos: 2/4; fast threes: 3/8
TEMPO: slow twos: slow   fast threes: medium

PHRASING: slow twos: 1 2 / 2 2 / 3 2 / 4 2 / 5 2 / 6 2

  fast threes: 1 2 3 / 2 2 3 / 3 2 3 / 4 2 3 / 5 2 3 / 6 2 3

OPENING POSITION: Fifth position, right foot front. Arms are down by the sides (Illus. 1).

PREPARATION (ALL LEVELS): This preparation is the part of the exercise I call the "slow twos."

Counts 1 2: From the opening position, tendu the right foot to the front and raise the arms to the sides slightly above the shoulders, leading with the fingertips (Illus. 2). Feel the opposition of the hands to the top of the head by imagining a line of energy that goes from the palms of both hands, through both arms to the spine, then up the spine and out the top of the head. The energy courses along this path, extending out the palms of the hands and out the top of the head.

Counts 2 2: Plié in fourth position, weight evenly distributed between both feet. Arms sweep down and cross at the wrists in front of you (Illus. 3).

EXERCISE 9
Illustration 1

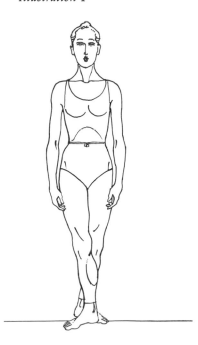

Counts 3 2: Lift to relevé and raise the arms up to the sides, as they were in count 1 (Illus. 4). Feel the opposition between the top of the head and the hands.

Counts 4 2: Plié in fourth position again and cross your arms at the wrist in front of you (Illus. 3).

Counts 5 2: Tendu the front foot, lifting to straighten the standing leg. Arms come back up to the sides and the weight should now be on the standing leg, as in count 1 (Illus. 2).

Counts 6 2: Close back to fifth position and plié. Arms cross at the wrists in front of you.

Repeat, taking the tendu with the right foot to the right side instead of the front (counts 1 and 5), and taking the plié (counts 2 and 4) and the relevé (count 3) in second position rather than fourth. As you finish, close to fifth position with the right foot in back. The arms remain the same.

Repeat, this time taking the tendu with the right foot to the back (count 1 and 5), and taking the plié (counts 2 and 4) and the relevé (count 3) again in fourth position. Close the right foot in back when you close to fifth. The arms remain the same.

Repeat again to the right side, closing back.

Now, starting with the left foot, repeat the slow twos to the front, left, back, and again to the left.

EXERCISE 9
Illustrations 2–4

2.   3.   4.

SEQUENCE:
Tendu with the right foot: front, right, back, right (close right foot back in fifth),
Tendu with the left foot: front, left, back, left (close left foot back in fifth).

This preparation can be done as a separate exercise. It is also always done as a preparation for each level of the fast threes exercise, to practice placement and to help you find equal oppositions throughout the body. Finding equal oppositional pulls will be particularly important in the intermediate and advanced versions.

When doing the slow twos try to accomplish the movement in as smooth a manner as possible. A good way to check yourself on this is to do the exercise first to music and then turn the music off and try to keep an internal sense of momentum and even flow as you do the exercise.

ELEMENTARY

The addition of the body is the fast threes part of the exercise. When the body is added the tempo changes from slow to medium and the meter changes to threes.

Begin by doing the slow twos once through to the right. Then change to the medium tempo.

Counts 1 2 3: Tendu the right foot to the front and raise the arms to the sides.

Counts 2 2 3: Plié in fourth position, weight evenly distributed between both feet. Take the head, shoulders, chest and part of the waist over forward. Simultaneously, the arms sweep down and cross in front of you (Illus. 5, solid lines). Be sure to maintain the lift in the high point, which is now in your lower back.

Counts 3 2 3: Successively roll the spine up to vertical, lifting in the body to straighten the legs. As the spine comes up to vertical, the high point travels up the spine. The arms lift to the sides and the upper back arches slightly. The high point is now reaching upward from the chest. Use the arch to take the whole body into relevé (Illus. 5, dotted lines). Be sure the hips and the weight remain evenly placed between both legs. Suspend the relevé.

Counts 4 2 3: Plié in fourth position and take the body and arms over, as in count 2. Be sure to bring the body through vertical before going forward.

Counts 5 2 3: Successively roll the spine up to vertical, lifting the body to straighten the legs, and tendu to the front. The arms lift to the sides (Illus. 2).

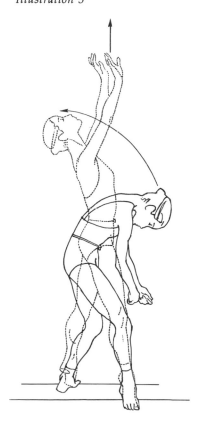

EXERCISE 9
Illustration 5

Counts 6 2 3: Close to fifth position and plié. The arms come down and cross at the wrists.

Repeat to the side, as follows:

Counts 1 2 3: From the fifth position plié, tendu the right foot directly to the right side, straightening the standing leg. Keep the body vertical and lift the arms to the sides, as in the slow twos.

Counts 2 2 3: Plié in second position and take the body directly over to the right side (Illus. 6, solid lines). The focus remains front and the arms sweep down to cross at the wrists. Lift from the high point in the left side of the ribcage.

Counts 3 2 3: Roll the spine back up through vertical and take the upper body directly over into a side bend to the left, lifting the arms to the sides. Use the lift in the high point, now in the right side of the ribcage, to straighten the legs and lift into relevé (Illus. 6, dotted lines).

Counts 4 2 3: Plié in second position with the body in a side bend to the right, arms sweeping down, as in count 2.

Counts 5 2 3: Roll the spine successionally back up to vertical, letting the lift straighten your legs, and tendu the right foot to the side. Your hips will be over the standing leg. Bring your arms up to the sides, as in count 1.

Counts 6 2 3: Close to fifth, right foot in back, and plié.

Repeat to the back, as follows:

Counts 1 2 3: As you lift from the fifth position plié, tendu the right foot back. Keep the body vertical and lift the arms to the sides.

Counts 2 2 3: Plié in fourth position and take an arch in the upper back, lifting from the high point in the chest. (Be sure to arch in the upper back only; taking the arch in the lower back will strain it.) Bring the arms down to cross in front of you (Illus. 7, solid lines).

Counts 3 2 3: Roll the upper body back up to vertical and take it directly over to the front. Keep lifting from the high point, now in the lower back, to straighten the legs and lift into relevé. Lift the arms up to the sides (Illus. 7, dotted lines).

Counts 4 2 3: Bring your body through vertical first, then lift the upper back into an arch as you plié in fourth position. The arms come down and cross in front.

Counts 5 2 3: Roll the spine back up to vertical, straightening the legs, and tendu the right foot back as you lift the arms up to the sides.

Counts 6 2 3: Close to fifth position and plié, right foot back, arms sweeping down and across.

Repeat to the right side.

Repeat the slow twos, front, side, back and side, beginning with the left foot. Then add the fast threes, beginning to the left.

6.   7.

SEQUENCE:
Slow twos with the right foot: front, side, back, side,
Fast threes with the right foot: front, side, back, side,
Slow twos with the left foot: front, side, back, side,
Fast threes with the left foot: front, side, back, side.

When you add the body you are adding the sixth point of opposition: the traveling high point. As the body moves off the vertical axis the traveling high point pairs in opposition with the head, with each hand and with each foot.

INTERMEDIATE

PURPOSE: To develop an awareness of how to use all the points of opposition, to practice using rebound to accomplish the lift in the body and to find and use the moment of suspension to release the working leg.

The intermediate version is identical to the elementary with one exception. Each time you lift into relevé, allow the body to go over just a bit farther and lift from the high point just a bit more in order to release the foot of the working leg off the floor slightly. Keep the hips in place. Try to achieve the sensation of being suspended on one leg for a split second. You will find that if your weight is evenly distributed between your legs and the working foot is suspended slightly off the floor, your standing leg will not really be supporting you for that split second. Imagine yourself suspended from a string attached to the high point (see the arrows in Illus. 8, 9 and 10). If you feel equal oppositional pulls between your hands, head, feet and high point, you will be better able to sense and hold the suspension.

EXERCISE 9
Illustrations 8–10

8.   9.   10.

SEQUENCE:
Slow twos with the right foot: front, side, back, side,
Fast threes with the right foot: front, side, back, side,
Slow twos with the left foot: front, side, back, side,
Fast threes with the left foot: front, side, back, side.

An image that might help you to get the sensation of suspension in the released foot, and to keep it from flying up and throwing you off balance, is to think of that foot as a magnet that continues to pull toward the floor as the body lifts it off the floor.

ADVANCED

PURPOSE: The intention of the advanced version is to achieve a "double suspension" and to add a swing in the upper body. As the swing is added, the upper body moves around the vertical axis while the lift at the high point maintains the vertical axis.

The advanced version is the same as the intermediate version with the addition of an upper body swing. It is best to do the advanced version without the release of the foot in relevé until you are comfortable with the swing in the body. When you feel secure with the changes in the body, release the foot in relevé.

Begin the advanced version by doing the slow twos all the way through to the right.

Then do the fast threes as follows. Begin with the right foot, tendu to the front.

Counts 1 2 3: Tendu front with the right foot, arms up. The body stays vertical.

Counts 2 2 3: Plíe in fourth position. The body goes over to the front, arms down (Illus. 5, solid lines).

Counts 3 2 3: Swing the body to the right, and then use the lift in the body along the vertical axis and at the high point to straighten the legs; continue the swing to the back. The arms rise to the sides and remain up as the arch in the upper back lifts the body into relevé. This is the moment at which you can increase the lift in order to suspend the movement. (The moment when the body swings from the side to the back is the point at which the front foot can release.)

Counts 4 2 3: As the upper body continues the swing to the left, the right foot is placed back down, and the heels lower through straight legs. The right arm curves over the head as the body continues to swing over to the front. Both arms come down.

Counts 5 2 3: Roll the spine back up to vertical and tendu to the front. The arms go up to the sides. Feel the oppositional pulls in the body.

Counts 6 2 3: The body remains vertical as you close to fifth and plié, arms sweeping down in front.

Beginning with the tendu to the right side, add the body as follows:

Counts 1 2 3: The body remains vertical and the arms go up to the sides as you tendu to the right side.

Counts 2 2 3: Drop the body over to the right (toward the working leg) as you plié in second position. The arms drop down.

Counts 3 2 3: Swing the body forward and use the lift in the body to straighten the legs. The arms go up to the sides. Continue the body swing to the left side, lifting into relevé, and sense the suspension in the high point in the right side of the ribcage. (This is the point at which the right foot can release.) Be sure to keep the hips centered.

Counts 4 2 3: Continue the body swing into an upper back arch. The moment of suspension in the arch is the moment of "double suspension" (from the suspension in the side bend to the suspension in the arch). Allow the foot to come down on the second beat of the measure (on count 2 of 4 2 3). Arms remain up to the sides.

Counts 5 2 3: Continue the upper body swing to the right side. The heels lower through straight legs and the left arm curves over the head. As the body continues to swing forward, the arms come down. Roll the spine back up to vertical, straightening the legs, and lift the arms up to the sides as you tendu to the right.

Counts 6 2 3: The body remains vertical as you close to fifth position and plié, right foot back, arms sweeping down in front.

Beginning with the tendu to the back, add the body as follows:

Counts 1 2 3: The body remains vertical and the arms go up to the sides as you tendu to the back.

Counts 2 2 3: The body lifts into an upper back arch as you plié in fourth position. Drop the arms down.

Counts 3 2 3: Swing the body toward the right side, lifting to straighten the legs, and continue to swing over to the front, lifting into relevé. The arms go up to the sides. (The lift into relevé is the point at which the back foot can release.)

Counts 4 2 3: Continue the body swing toward the left and then back into an arch. The foot remains released and the hips stay centered.

Counts 5 2 3: The body continues to swing toward the right, the left arm curves over the head, and the released foot comes back down to the floor. The heels lower through straight legs. The body swings forward and both arms come down. Roll the spine back up to vertical and, straightening the legs, lift the arms to the sides as you tendu to the back.

Counts 6 2 3: The body remains vertical as you close to fifth position and plié, arms sweeping down in front.

SEQUENCE:
Slow twos with the right foot: front, side, back, side,
Fast threes with the right foot: front, side, back, side,
Slow twos with the left foot: front, side, back, side,
Fast threes with the left foot: front, side, back, side.

In order to accomplish the advanced version, you must try to maintain the lift through the spine, which will give you the necessary freedom in the upper torso. Always keep your hips and weight evenly placed between both legs—even when the support is only on one leg for that brief moment of suspension when the foot is released.

Always be sure that the relevé comes from the lift in the body rather than from the legs pushing the body up. This helps to keep the hips aligned.

It will help you to keep your balance if you think of your body lifting along the vertical axis (or from the high point) at all times, regardless of which way your upper body is curving. This also helps to keep the weight lifted out of the legs.

Once you have started the body swing, just keep the momentum going. If you try to stop in any position, you will throw yourself off balance.

Though lifts and suspensions are emphasized here, keep in mind that there is always weight in the legs and that the body is always connected to the ground through the legs.

ADVANCED VARIATION

Add a half turn on counts 3 2 3 and another half turn on counts 4 2 3. Always turn in the direction that your body is going. You will find that the momentum for the turn comes from the swing in the body.

NOTES TO TEACHERS

As you teach the slow twos (the preparation), try stopping the music in the middle of the exercise and letting the class continue in silence. This should help them learn to keep the rhythm going internally and to sense how the body can reflect the quality of the music on its own.

One way to help students keep track of the tempo internally during the slow twos is to subdivide the beat as you count out loud to them:

1 & 2 & 3 & and so forth throughout the exercise; or

1 & ah 2 & ah 3 & ah; or

1 2 3 4 5 6 / 2 2 3 4 5 6 / 3 2 3 4 5 6 /

You can also alternate the subdivisions within the exercise.

In the intermediate version, try holding the student's foot as it releases during the suspension. This will help the student feel the oppositional pull between the released foot as it reaches toward the floor and the lift from the high point in the spine.

Have students take a breath on counts 2 3 of the third measure and 2 3 of the fourth measure to help them feel the suspension and to help them with the balance.

Labanotation for this exercise is provided on page 196.

The metronome setting for this exercise is ♩ = 60 for the slow twos and ♩. = 63 for the fast threes.

Phrasing for musical accompaniment:

Slow Twos

1 2 / 2 2 / 3 2 / 4 2 / 5 2 / 6 2

Fast Threes

1 2 3 / 2 2 3 / 3 2 3 / 4 2 3 / 5 2 3 / 6 2 3

TEN: FOOT ISOLATIONS

PURPOSE: If you have accomplished Exercises One through Nine, the upper body should be totally warm. It is time to give the body a rest and concentrate on warming up the legs. Designed to warm up the ankles and feet, this is also an exercise in changing accents.

The foot isolations are really not an integral part of the technique. I have added them so that students can realign and recenter the body and work on coordination at the same time as they are warming up the ankles and feet before proceeding.

METER: 4/4
TEMPO: medium

PHRASING: 1 2 3 4 / 5 6 7 8 / 1 2 3 4 & / 5 & 6 & 7 & 8

OPENING POSITION: Standing in first position, arms down at the sides.

ALL LEVELS

EXERCISE 10
Illustration 1

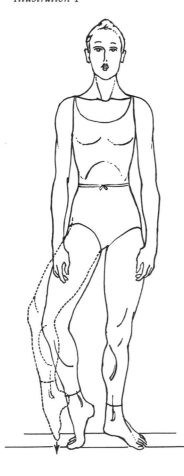

Count 1: Lift the right heel off the floor, leaving the ball of the foot and the toes on the floor (Illus. 1, solid lines).

Count 2: Use the toes to push the foot up and slightly off the floor, but not away from the body (Illus. 1, dotted lines).

Count 3: Bring the toes and the ball of the foot back to the floor, leaving the heel lifted, as in count 1.

Count 4: Place the heel and foot on the floor, in first position.

Counts 5 6 7 8: Repeat counts 1 through 4.

The next counts 1 through 8 are accomplished smoothly.

Count 1: Lift the right heel, then push the ball of the foot and the toes off the floor in 1 count.

Count 2: Place the toes, the ball of the foot and the heel back on the floor—in that order—in 1 count.

Count 3: Repeat count 1.

Count 4: Repeat count 2.

Accent the upbeats on counts 1 and 3. In the next 4 counts, the & counts are used to create an accent on the downbeat.

Count &: Push the foot off (as in count 1 above).

Count 5: Place the toes, ball and heel on the floor (as in count 2 above).

Count &: Foot off.

Count 6: Foot down.

Count &: Foot off.

Count 7: Foot down.

Count &: Foot off.

Count 8: Foot down.

Repeat the exercise, two sets of 8 counts, with the left foot.

Then repeat the entire exercise, adding successional arms: the arms lift (as if pulling off a sweater) and then open out to the sides in the first 8 counts; then the arms reverse, closing in on the second 8 counts. This is an exercise in coordination in which the arms must move smoothly and continuously as the feet move in accented phrases.

SEQUENCE:
First set of counts 1 through 8 on the right,
Second set of counts 1 through 8 on the right,
First set of counts 1 through 8 on the left,
Second set of counts 1 through 8 on the left,
First and second sets on the right with arms,
First and second sets on the left with arms.

NOTES TO TEACHERS

This is not strictly a Limón exercise; it is here simply for the purpose of warming up the ankles. I have added successional arms to help with coordination: the smooth quality in the arms in contrast to the staccato quality in the legs.

The body can also be added to this: add a successional roll up to an arch in 8 counts, and a successional roll down in 8 counts.

Labanotation for this exercise is provided on page 198.

The metronome setting for this exercise is ♩ = 116.
Phrasing for musical accompaniment:

1 2 3 4 / 5 6 7 8 / 1 2 3 4 & / 5 & 6 & 7 & 8

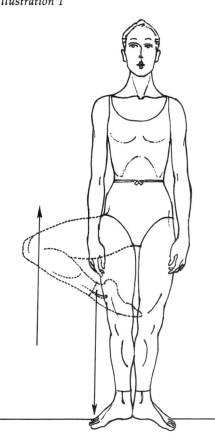

ELEVEN: PASSÉ SERIES

PURPOSE: To rest the body, briefly, and to check that the body is centered after the off-center work in Exercise Nine.

This is another exercise that is not integral to the style, but it's helpful at this point to check your centering while keeping the legs warm.

METER: 4/4
TEMPO: fast

PHRASING: 4 / 1̇ 2 3 4 / 2̇ 2 3 4 / 3̇ 2 3 4 / 4̇ 2 3 4

OPENING POSITION: Standing in first position, arms down at the sides.

PREPARATION (ALL LEVELS): With both legs turned out, lift the toes of the right foot to the left knee, keeping the weight evenly distributed between the hips (Illus. 1). This will cause you to start to fall toward the right side. Allow yourself to fall and catch yourself. Try it several times with each leg and try to sense the placement of your hips underneath your shoulders as you passé each leg without shifting your weight. As you go through the exercise try to maintain this alignment.

ELEMENTARY

This exercise has an accent on the downbeat: think "up" on 4, "down" on 1, and lift in the body throughout.

Count 4: From the opening position, lift the right leg to passé, keeping both legs turned out.

Counts 1 2 3: Bring the right foot back down to first position on count 1 and use counts 2 3 to continue to lengthen the legs and lengthen in the spine.

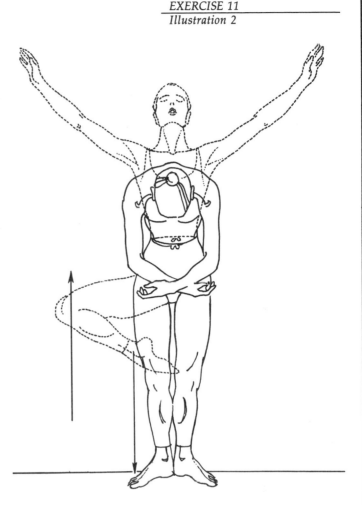

Do this 4 times with the right leg, 4 times with the left leg, 2 right, 2 left, 1 right, 1 left, 1 right, 1 left.

Repeat the entire exercise, adding successional arms as follows: as the right leg comes to passé 4 times, the arms rise and open out to the sides in 4 counts. The arms curve and close in, in 4 counts, as the left leg comes to passé 4 times. Then the arms rise and open out to the sides in 2 counts as the right leg comes to passé twice. They curve and close in, in 2 counts, as the left leg comes to passé twice. Finally, the arms rise and open out on 1 count as the right leg comes to passé once, and they close in 1 count as the left leg comes to passé once.

SEQUENCE:
4 passés right leg,
4 passés left leg,
2 passés right,
2 passés left,
Passé once: right, left, right, left; then
4 passés right: arms open,
4 passés left: arms close,
2 passés right: arms open,
2 passés left: arms close,
Passé once right, left, right, left: arms open
with right leg, close with left leg.

Then repeat the entire passé series with arms,
this time beginning with the left leg. The sequence stays the same,
but the arms will open as you passé with the left foot and close as
you passé with the right.

The arms should move as smoothly as possible, creating a contrast
between the flow of the arms and the accent in the legs.

INTERMEDIATE

The body is added in the intermediate version. The opening position is slightly different: Stand in first position, arms down at the sides. Take your head, shoulders, chest and part of your waist over forward (Illus. 2, solid lines).

As you take the 4 passés with the right leg, successively roll the spine up to vertical and into an upper body arch. With the rolling up in the spine allow the arms to rise. Open the arms out to the sides as you arch (Illus. 2, dotted lines).

As you take the 4 passés with the left leg, bring the body back to vertical and then over to the front, simultaneously closing the arms in and down. You should finish in the opening position.

Repeat the same action in the body and arms as you passé twice with each leg, and then once with each leg.

SEQUENCE:
4 passés right: body arches, arms open,
4 passés left: body over, arms in,
2 passés right: body arches, arms open,
2 passés left: body over, arms in,
Passé once right, left, right, left: body arches, arms open with right leg passés, body over, arms in with left leg passés.

Then repeat the passé series beginning with the left leg. The body and arm sequence stays the same, but this time as you passé with the left leg the spine will roll up and the arms will open, and as you passé with the right leg the body will go over and the arms will close in.

Be sure to maintain the lift in the high point as it travels up and down the spine.

ADVANCED

Quarter, half and full turns are added in the advanced version. Practice the turns first before adding the body and arms. Begin in the opening position and push the right foot up and off the floor. As you lift the knee into passé, use the momentum of that movement to turn a quarter turn to the right. This should all happen on count 4 (the first count). Bring the foot back down to first position and finish the turn on count 1. The push of the foot off the floor begins the turn and the opening of the knee into passé completes it.

Do 4 quarter turns to the right, bringing the right leg to passé; then 4 to the left with the left leg. Then try it with half turns, 2 to the right and 2 to the left. Finally, try full turns, 1 to the right, 1 left, 1 right and 1 left. Each time, the passé and the turn will happen on count 4, and the foot will come to first position on count 1. You will have to release the heel of the standing leg slightly off the floor in order to turn, but you should not go all the way into relevé. Use counts – 2 3 to lengthen in the spine.

Once you have mastered the turns, add the arms. The arms will open as you do 4 quarter turns to the right, close as you do 4 quarter turns to the left. They will open as you do half turns to the right, close as you do half turns to the left. The arms open on the full turn to the right, close on the full turn to the left.

Once you are comfortable with the turns and the arms, add the body: unroll the spine as the arms open, take the body over as the arms close. You can slow the tempo down a bit as you do the half and full turns, in order to accommodate the movement in the body.

SEQUENCE:
4 passés right, plain quarter turns,
4 passés left, plain quarter turns,
2 passés right, plain half turns,
2 passés left, plain half turns,
Passé with plain full turn once: right, left, right, left.

Repeat the series with turns beginning with the left leg.

Then add the arms, and go once through the series beginning the passés with the right leg and once through beginning left. When you begin the series to the left, the arms will open with the left leg and close with the right.

Next, add the body to the arms and turns: once through the series to the right and once to the left. When you begin the series with the left leg, the arms will open and the body will arch with the left leg and reverse with the right.

Whenever the body is in action, whether or not you are turning, it is the lift in the high point that keeps you on center.

NOTES TO TEACHERS

Try using this image: Each time the foot lifts to the knee, imagine air being pumped into the body (like a bicycle pump), which helps the arms to open a little more with each passé.

Labanotation for this exercise is provided on page 198.

The metronome setting for this exercise is ♩ = 144.
Phrasing for musical accompaniment:

4 / 1 2 3 4 / 1 2 3 4 / 1 2 3 4 / 1 2 3 4

TWELVE: Developpé Series

PURPOSE: To lengthen the legs in developpé and to work on one-leg balances as the body goes off center.

José would do developpés at the barre with many variations on the body, arms and dynamics. I took out the changes in dynamics and the variations in order to concentrate on the continuous flow of the movement and on the elongation of the muscles. I have also taken this exercise away from the barre so that you have to use centering and alignment to hold your balance. I have found that, away from the barre, it is best to alternate the working leg to the front, to the side, to the back and to the side, in

EXERCISE 12
Illustrations 1–3

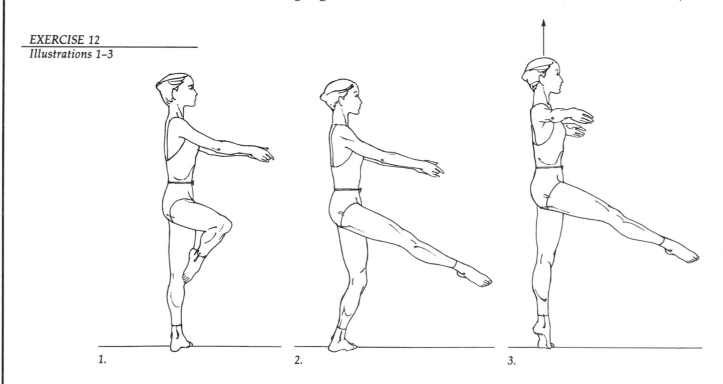

1. 2. 3.

order to work on balance and to prevent the standing leg from tiring.

METER: 4/4
TEMPO: medium

PHRASING: 1 2 3 4 5 6 7 8

OPENING POSITION: Standing in first position, arms down at the sides.

ELEMENTARY

Counts 1 2: Passé the right leg by drawing the toes up the side of the leg to the knee. Keep the hips stable and keep both legs turned out. At the same time, bring the arms up to first position: the arms are rounded in front of the body, chest height, fingertips almost touching. The palms of the hands should be about a foot in front of the chest (Illus. 1).

Counts 3 4: Extend (developpé) the right leg forward, leading with the foot and keeping both legs turned out. Use the foot to draw the leg out and stretch it straight in front of you. (The leg can be extended at a 45-degree angle to the floor, or lower. It is not the height of the leg that is most important. You are working on balance, the placement of the hips and the stretch in the leg.) At the same time, plié the standing leg and extend both arms in front of you, leading with the fingertips (Illus. 2). Time the movement so that the arms and leg finish lengthening at the same time. Be sure to keep your shoulders aligned over your hips.

Counts 5 6: Beginning with the top of the head, lift the body and stretch the spine so that the standing leg straightens underneath you. Try not to push up from your foot; use the body lift to straighten the leg. Keep the lift going into relevé and feel the chest open, which will cause the arms to draw in toward the chest slightly. Use the opening of the chest to allow the arms to open successively to the sides (shoulders, elbows, wrists, fingertips). You should now be in a high balance, at the peak of the movement, and ready to send your weight forward (Illus. 3).

Count 7: Take your hips and body forward and step onto the right leg. Plié the right leg and allow the left leg to release off the floor and stretch behind you (Illus. 4).

Count 8: Lift to straighten the standing leg and close into first position. Bring the arms down.

Repeat, starting with the left foot.

Repeat the exercise again with the right foot, taking

EXERCISE 12
Illustration 4

the developpé to the right side and stepping to the right; with the left foot, taking the developpé to the left side and stepping to the left; then with the right foot, taking the developpé to the back and stepping to the back; and with the left foot, taking the developpé to the back and stepping to the back; finally, take the developpé to both sides again. The movement in the arms remains the same throughout: they reach forward as the leg extends, open successively to the side as you relevé, and come down as you close to first position.

SEQUENCE:
Developpé front: right, left,
Developpé side: right, left,
Developpé back: right, left,
Developpé side: right, left.

When taking the developpé to the side, try to keep the hip of the standing leg directly over the foot as you relevé (Illus. 5). Think of the top of the head stretching upward.

When extending the leg to the back, be sure to keep the shoulders

EXERCISE 12
Illustrations 5–7

5. 6. 7.

directly over the hips, and the hips directly over the standing leg (Illus. 6). Thinking of the points of opposition in the body will help you keep your balance and maintain the alignment.

The whole exercise should be accomplished as smoothly as possible. You may find that it is easier to do the exercise at a faster tempo. Try it that way until you are comfortable with it, then slow it down. Your goal is to find the balance and continuous flow of the movement at the medium tempo, which is the more difficult. Keep the leg at a comfortable height.

As you reach the peak of the movement—each time you lift into relevé—think of the oppositions in the body. The equal pull at each point of opposition helps you to maintain your balance without straining or pushing.

INTERMEDIATE AND ADVANCED

The legs and arms are the same as in the elementary version. The body is now added.

Counts 1 2: Passé the right leg, bringing the arms up to first position.

Counts 3 4: As you developpé the leg, bringing the arms forward, and plié on the standing leg, take the body over forward, leading with the top of the head. Feel the upward stretch in the high point (between the shoulder blades) and through the vertical axis. This will help you keep your balance (Illus. 7).

Count 5: Roll the spine up to vertical and lift through the high point, which is now in the top of the head, to straighten the standing leg. Bring the arms in slightly toward your chest.

Count 6: Arch in the upper back and lift in the body to relevé, lowering the extended leg. The chest opens and the arms extend successively out to the sides (Illus. 7). The high point has now moved down and is reaching upward from the chest. As you reach the peak of the movement, you should be in a suspended high balance with the hips aligned over the standing leg.

Count 7: Step forward onto the right foot, maintaining the arch as you take your body forward. Roll the spine up to vertical as you step into the plié. Release and stretch the back leg behind you.

Count 8: Lift to straighten the standing leg, close to first position, and bring the arms down.

Repeat with the left leg.

EXERCISE 12
Illustration 8

Now take the developpé to the side with the right leg, and add the body as follows:

Counts 1 2: Passé the right leg, bringing the arms up to first position.

Counts 3 4: Developpé the right leg to the right side and take the body in a side bend to the right. Plié on the left leg. The arms extend forward (Illus. 8, solid lines).

Count 5: Roll the spine successively up to vertical, straightening the standing leg, and begin to open the arms successively out to the sides. Feel the opposition between the head and the extended foot as the foot reaches toward the floor.

Count 6: Take the body over into a side bend away from the standing leg (toward the left) as you lift into relevé. The arms continue to open. Again, feel the oppositional pull between the top of the head and the extended foot (Illus. 8, dotted lines). This will help you maintain your balance.

Count 7: Step onto the right foot, releasing the left foot, and roll the spine up to vertical as you plié.

Count 8: Lift to straighten the standing leg, and close to first position. Bring the arms down.

Repeat with the left leg extending to the left side.

Now take the developpé to the back with the right leg, and add the body as follows:

Counts 1 2: Passé the right leg, bringing the arms up to the first position.

Counts 3 4: Developpé the right leg behind you, extend the arms forward, and plié on the standing leg as you lift the upper back into an arch (Illus. 9, solid lines).

Count 5: Roll the spine successively up to vertical, straightening the standing leg.

Count 6: Take the head, shoulders, chest and waist over forward as you lift into relevé, lowering the extended leg. The arms open successionally out to the sides. Again, feel the oppositional pull between the top of the head and the extended foot (Illus. 9, dotted lines).

Count 7: Step back onto the right foot, releasing the left foot in front of you, and plié as you roll the spine back up to vertical.

Count 8: Lift to straighten the standing leg, and close to first position. Bring the arms down.

Repeat with the left leg extending to the back. Then repeat the developpés to each side.

Daniel Lewis teaching at the Juilliard School.

PETER SCHAAF

SEQUENCE:
Developpé front with arms and body; right leg, left leg,
Developpé side with arms and body; right leg, left leg,
Developpé back with arms and body; right leg, left leg,
Developpé side with arms and body; right leg, left leg.

NOTES TO TEACHERS

Stress the continuity of the movement and the use of the oppositional pulls to help maintain balance. The exercise can be performed without the arms as a way of testing balance—students often use the arms to balance the body, rather than using the body to balance.

As they relevé (on counts 5 6), have the students take a deep breath to help with balance and to give the peak of the movement—the relevé—an extra lift. Do this no more than two times in succession.

If students are having trouble with the balance, have them try it at the barre so they can feel the moment of lift and balance, and then have them find that moment on their own in the center.

Be sure that hips are always properly aligned over the standing leg.
Labanotation for this exercise is provided on page 200.

The metronome setting for this exercise is ♩ = 56.
Phrasing for musical accompaniment:

1 2 3 4 / 5 6 7 8

THIRTEEN: LUNGE SERIES

PURPOSE: To transfer the weight from one leg to the other, taking the weight off center with a fall and using the successional lift in the body to bring the weight back on center. This is accomplished without the aid of rebound.

This exercise is presented basically the way José taught it. I have added the turn in the advanced version and the flexed hands, rather than the extended hands that José used, to help you feel the oppositions, keep your shoulders down and feel the length in the muscles along the ribs.

METER: 4/4
TEMPO: medium

PHRASING: 1 2 3 & 4

OPENING POSITION: Standing in fifth position, right foot in front, arms down at the sides.

ELEMENTARY

Count 1: Brush the right foot forward along the floor, allowing the toes to come off the floor (this is called a "dégagé"), as you raise the arms and extend them to the sides, above shoulder height (Illus. 1). Feel an equal oppositional pull between the head, both hands and both feet. This is the moment at which you should feel the greatest potential energy.

Count 2: With the right leg take a long lunge forward into a plié. Keep both legs turned out. The left foot should stay on the floor, though the heel can come off slightly. Keep the left leg stretched behind you. The body stays vertical, hips and shoulders square to the front, focus forward. Bring your arms down to cross at the wrists in front of you (Illus. 2). This is a case in which the leg is falling, or giving in to gravity, so sense the weight in the leg as you lunge forward.

Count 3: Bring your hips back over the standing (left) leg, keeping the standing leg straight. Allow the right leg to straighten and then push off the floor lightly with the right foot. Simultaneously, swing the arms back up to the sides, leading with the fingertips.

Count &: Lifting from the top of the head, relevé on the left leg, keeping the right leg extended in front of you, toes pointed. The arms will lift slightly—use the lift in the arms and the top of the head to sense the suspension in the relevé. This is the peak of the movement. All oppositional pulls should be equal at this point.

Count 4: Release the oppositions. (Imagine that the pull on the strings attached to your hands, head and feet is slackened.) Lower the left heel and close to fifth position plié as you lower your arms.

Repeat, again with the right foot, this time taking the dégagé and lunge to the right side, bringing the hips back over the standing left leg, and closing the right foot back in fifth position. Then with the right foot again, take the dégagé and lunge to the back; and again to the right side. Close the right foot in back as you finish in fifth position so that the left foot is in front to begin the lunges to the left.

SEQUENCE:
Lunge to the front, right foot,
Lunge to the right, right foot
   (close right foot back),
Lunge to the back, right foot,
Lunge to the right, right foot
   (close right foot back);
Lunge to the front, left foot,
Lunge to the left, left foot
   (close left foot back),
Lunge to the back, left foot,
Lunge to the left, left foot
   (close left foot back).

Proper alignment is very important for balance in this exercise. Be sure to keep both hips square to the front and the shoulders placed over the hips.

Always begin the relevé by lifting with the top of the head and with the body.

This exercise is an opportunity to practice using the

EXERCISE 13
Illustration 2

oppositions to help you stretch and lengthen your muscles. Feel an equal pull between the top of the head, the right hand, the right foot, the left hand and the left foot. Each time you come into fifth position plié, release the oppositional pulls gently.

INTERMEDIATE

The legs and arms are the same as in the elementary version. In the intermediate version you will add the body.

Count 1: Dégagé the right foot front, brushing the foot along the floor. The arms come up to the sides and the body stays vertical.

Count 2: Lunge forward into plié on the right leg, and beginning with the top of the head, drop the head, shoulders, chest, waist and hips over to the front. The arms come down and cross at the wrists (Illus. 3, solid lines). Remember to use the weight of the head in the fall and to keep lifting in the high point, which is now in the lower back, as the body goes over.

Count 3: Bring the hips back over the standing leg by starting the movement in the hips and releasing the right foot off the floor. (Keep the toes reaching toward the floor, as if they were being pulled by a magnet.) Continue the movement in the lumbar and roll the spine successively up to vertical as the arms swing up to the sides. The high point travels up the spine and into the top of the head. Use this lift to take you into a relevé suspension as the body rolls up. Keep the right leg extended in front of you (Illus. 3, dotted lines).

Count &: Keep the relevé going and the arms lifting. Use the oppositional pull between the head, hands and feet to achieve the quality of suspension in the relevé.

Count 4: Releasing the oppositions, lower the heel and close into fifth position plié, at the same time bringing the arms down.

Repeat, taking the dégagé to the right side and the drop in the body to the right; then take the dégagé to the back, with an arch in the body; repeat to the side, and close the right foot in back into fifth position plié. Repeat the exercise on the left. The arm movements are the same throughout.

SEQUENCE:
Lunge front, right foot, body over,
Lunge right, right foot, body to the side
  (close right foot back).
Lunge back, right foot, body arch,

EXERCISE 13
Illustration 3

Lunge right, right foot, body to the side
   (close right foot back);
Lunge front, left foot, body over,
Lunge left, left foot, body to the left
   (close left foot back),
Lunge back, left foot, body arch,
Lunge left, left foot, body to the left
   (close left foot back).

ADVANCED

The advanced version is the same as the intermediate, with the addition of half turns.

Count 1: Dégagé the right foot front, brushing the foot along the floor. The arms come up to the sides.

Count 2: Lunge forward into plié on the right leg, and beginning with the top of the head, drop the head, shoulders, chest, waist and hips over to the front. The arms come down and cross at the wrists.

Count 3: Bring the hips back over the standing leg and release the right foot off the floor. Begin to roll the spine successively up to vertical and start the arms swinging up to the sides. The half turn goes clockwise (toward the gesture leg) and begins just as your weight centers over the standing leg. The roll up of the spine keeps the momentum going. Put a little extra energy (more of a sensation than a big movement) into the right hand to help you use the momentum to turn to face back. Trust the momentum in your body—it will keep you turning as your spine rolls up. The peak of the movement occurs as you complete the turn, facing back.

Be sure to keep the alignment of the hips over the standing leg and the shoulders over the hips as you roll the spine up to vertical and as you turn. Time the roll up in the spine so that you reach vertical and relevé as you complete the turn.

Count &: Keep the relevé going and the arms lifting. Use the oppositional pull between the head, hands and feet to achieve the quality of suspension in the relevé.

Count 4: Releasing the oppositions, lower the heel and close to fifth position plié, bringing the arms down.

Continue by taking the lunge with the right leg and the side bend to the right side, and make a half turn counterclockwise (toward the standing leg) to face front. Close the right foot back in fifth position plié. Try to keep the hips properly aligned as you turn with the side bend.

Repeat, taking the lunge to the back with an arch in the body, and turning counterclockwise (toward the standing leg) to face back. Then take the lunge to the right side, with a side bend to the right, and turn counterclockwise to face front. Close the right foot back in fifth position plié, ready to begin the sequence with the left foot.

SEQUENCE:
Lunge front, right foot, body over,
  half turn to the right
Lunge right, right foot, body to the right,
  half turn to the left, close back in fifth;
Lunge back, right foot, body arch,
  half turn to the left,
Lunge right, right foot, body to the right,
  half turn to the left, close back in fifth;
Lunge front, left foot, body over,
  half turn to the left,
Lunge left, left foot, body to the left,
  half turn to the right, close back in fifth;
Lunge back, left foot, body arch,
  half turn to the right,
Lunge left, left foot, body to the left,
  half turn to the right, close back in fifth.

ADVANCED VARIATION

The advanced version can be done with full turns.

NOTES TO TEACHERS

In the intermediate and advanced versions, the successional roll of the spine up to vertical should be timed so that it finishes at the last moment before the relevé. This helps to keep the momentum going in the turns.

In the intermediate version, make sure that the arms move continuously and fluidly. In the advanced version, though it is the body that initiates the lift and continues the movement, it is the continuous flow of the arms that controls the turns.

Labanotation for this exercise is provided on page 201.

The metronome setting for this exercise is ♩ = 46.
Phrasing for musical accompaniment:

FOURTEEN: SPIRAL TURNS

PURPOSE: To experience the contrasts between the sensations of fall and suspension. This is the first time that the entire body moves around a stationary vertical axis, rather than just the upper body as in previous exercises.

The elementary version of this exercise was originally taught by José as a complete exercise on its own. He also taught a floor exercise that used the spiral in the upper body in a series of swings. I have combined the two, using a spiral in the upper body to initiate a turn.

METER: 3/4
TEMPO: medium

PHRASING: 1 2 3 / 4 5 6

OPENING POSITION: Legs parallel, high relevé, arms stretching upward, focus front (Illus. 1, solid lines).

EXERCISE 14
Illustration 1

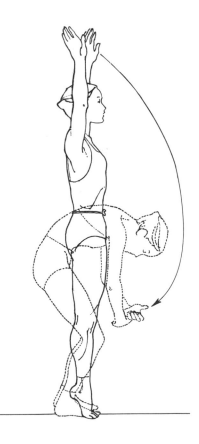

ELEMENTARY

The elementary version is used as a preparation for the intermediate and advanced versions, in which the turns are added. Use this version to warm up the spine and to feel the continuity and flow of the fall, rebound, stretch, plié, relevé and successional arms. In this particular exercise, any elementary students who are comfortable with the following version can go ahead and try the intermediate version with the turns.

Count 1: From the opening position, drop into plié. The upper body falls forward and the arms drop down (Illus. 1, dotted lines).

Count 2: Rebound to begin to bring the spine and the arms successionally up to vertical.

Count 3: Use the lift in the body to straighten the legs and to bring the arms overhead (Illus. 2, solid lines).

Count 4: Plié and arch in the upper back as you open the arms out to the sides (Illus. 2, dotted lines).

Count 5: Lift in the body to straighten the legs. The arms reach out and up.

Count 6: Continue the lift into relevé; the arms continue to reach upward.

Repeat at least 4 times. You can increase the tempo as you become more comfortable with the exercise. With the increase in tempo, the fall will happen more quickly, but try to keep the movement flowing evenly and continuously.

INTERMEDIATE

Do the elementary version 4 times as a preparation in order to start the momentum going and to feel the fall. Keep the body relaxed, using the oppositional pulls to stretch at the peak of the movement.

Counts 1 2 3 4: Same as the elementary version.

Count 5: Keeping the chest open and the arms stretching to the sides in opposition, lift the upper body into a high spiral to your right (a slight side bend with an arch), and start to take a half turn, going clockwise on the right foot. The chest, lifting in the arch, leads into the turn. The left foot reaches back and down as it releases off the floor to turn. This creates an opposition between the top of the head and the left foot. Think of this turn spiraling upward and suspending from the high point in the chest.

Count 6: Keep the high point lifting in the spiral as you complete the turn. Use the lift in the high point to relevé. This suspension is the peak of the movement (Illus. 3). The hips and shoulders swing around to the back and the legs come to parallel in order to complete the turn and prepare to fall. You should arrive in the fall by count 1 of the next phrase.

Repeat, continuing to go clockwise, taking another half turn so that you face front again. Repeat twice more, taking the spiral and the half turn counterclockwise to face back, and then once more counterclockwise to finish facing front.

SEQUENCE:
Repeat the elementary version 4 times; then
Fall, spiral, half turn clockwise,
Fall, spiral, half turn clockwise;
Fall, spiral, half turn counterclockwise,
Fall, spiral, half turn counterclockwise.

ADVANCED

The advanced version is the same as the intermediate, taking a full turn instead of a half turn. Begin by doing the full intermediate sequence. Then do the advanced version, with the full turns, 4 times: clockwise, counterclockwise, and repeat. Slow the tempo down slightly as you do the full turns.

SEQUENCE:
Repeat the elementary version 4 times;
Repeat the intermediate version 4 times:

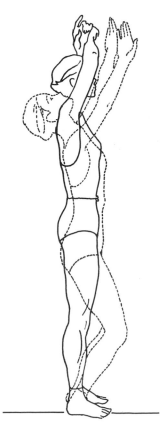

EXERCISE 14
Illustration 2

twice clockwise, twice counterclockwise; then
Full turn clockwise,
Full turn counterclockwise,
Full turn clockwise,
Full turn counterclockwise.

NOTES TO TEACHERS

As this is the first time that the entire body moves *around* a stationary vertical axis, try using an image to help clarify the idea of the body spiraling around the axis. At the beginning of the exercise, the body is lifted and vertical. Ask students to imagine that they are the central, vertical axis of a barbershop pole when they are standing in this position. Then, as they go into the spiral turn, ask them to imagine that their bodies have become the stripe on the pole, spiraling around and up the pole.

All oppositional pulls in the body must be equal during the turn in order to keep the body on balance in the off-center position. The tendency is to forget about the oppositional pull in the gesture leg as it lengthens to the back in the turn.

One of the main purposes of this exercise is to find the moment of suspension (on count 6) in the high spiral, just before the hips and shoulders come around into the fall. This quality of suspension is one of the distinctive elements of Limón technique, and though it is difficult to achieve, when properly accomplished it can give the illusion of defying gravity. One way to help students find this moment is to ritard the music at that point, slightly increasing the time for the suspension on count 6.

Labanotation for this exercise is provided on page 201.

The metronome setting for this exercise is $\downarrow. = 92$.
Phrasing for musical accompaniment:

For help with the suspension

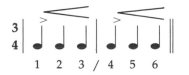

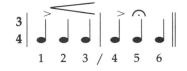

EXERCISE 14
Illustration 3

FIFTEEN: 12-COUNT PHRASE

PURPOSE: To combine and feel all the oppositional pulls as the body goes off center and comes back on center, and to feel the rebound and suspension, the isolation of the hip joint as it rotates in and rotates out, and the hip and shoulder alignment during the turn. This exercise combines all the elements of the technique learned thus far.

I have taken elements of four different exercises that José taught and combined them in this 12-count phrase, in which there is a turn (a pirouette) and the reverse of a back bend (the fall and successional roll up of the spine). José used to joke with us in the studio, saying, "Now I want six pirouettes with a back bend to the floor." This is my way of putting everything together and saying to José, "It *is* possible, I just can't give you the back bend, only a roll up from the floor."

EXERCISE 15
Illustration 1

METER: 3/4
TEMPO: medium
PHRASING: 1 2 3 / 4 5 6 / 7 8 9 / 10 11 12

OPENING POSITION: Wide second position, arms diagonally out to the sides, hands flexed (Illus. 1, solid lines).

PREPARATION # 1 (ALL LEVELS): This begins with the same type of fall and recovery as in Exercise Fourteen.

Count 1: Drop into plié in second position. The body falls over forward and the arms drop down and cross at the wrists (Illus. 1).

Count 2: Rebound in the legs and body.

Count 3: Use the rebound to start bringing the spine successionally up to vertical. Use the lift in the body to straighten the legs as you bring the arms successionally up to chest height and open them out to the sides.

Counts 4 5 6: Take all 3 counts to plié, sustaining the oppositional pulls in the arms as you deepen the plié and arch in the upper body. Sense the lift through the vertical axis (Illus. 2, solid lines).

Counts 7 8: Lift from the chest to straighten the legs. Continue the lift in the chest and take the weight onto the right leg as you rotate the shoulders and hips directly to the right. Allow the legs to turn parallel. Breaking at the hips, take the upper body over into a flat back (parallel to the floor, like a tabletop). The left leg stretches behind you, the toes touching the floor in a parallel tendu. The left arm stretches forward, parallel to the floor; the right arm stretches out to the side, parallel to the floor but at a right angle to the body. Be sure that both hips are well over the right leg (Illus. 2).

Count 9: Stretch in the flat-back position and feel the opposition of the left foot stretching to the floor and the left arm reaching forward. The more you stretch in this position, the greater the potential energy you will have in your body, and the more momentum the upper body will have in the swing. You will also be able to achieve more rotation in the hips.

Counts 10 11 12: Rotate the left hip and left leg back to the turned-out position so that both hips are evenly placed between both feet in second position, legs straight. At the same time, swing the body forward so that the head, shoulders, chest and waist are hanging over forward. The arms come down to the sides (Illus. 3, solid lines). You should arrive in this position right on the count of 10. The drop and swing in the body will create a rebound. Use the rebound to bring the spine successively up to vertical on counts 11 and 12 (Illus. 3, dotted lines). On count 11, the arms lift so that they are rounded in front of you, fingertips touching, and then the arms open to the side on count 12.

Repeat, this time rotating toward the left.

EXERCISE 15
Illustrations 2–3

2.

3.

EXERCISE 15
Illustration 4

SEQUENCE:
4 times: right, left, right, left.

PREPARATION # 2 (ALL LEVELS): Once you are comfortable with the first preparation, try allowing the momentum of the lift through the chest (counts 7 and 8) release the tendu foot behind you.

On count 9, as the body goes over into the tabletop position, keep the leg connected to the line of the body so that the foot and the leg release and lift behind you as a result of the movement in the body (Illus. 4, solid lines). Try to keep the leg parallel to the floor in the same plane as your upper body (think of your body, arms and leg as part of one long tabletop). Maintain the oppositional pull of the hand to the foot (left hand to left foot, or right hand to right foot). Really stretch in this position in order to feel the potential energy. Your body should have as much potential energy in this lateral stretch as it does in the vertical stretch of a high relevé.

On count 10 the foot comes down as the hip rotates. Allow the legs to plié in second position as the body swings and falls to center (Illus. 4).

Use the rebound to bring the spine successively up to vertical. At the same time lift to straighten the legs and open the arms on counts 11 and 12.

Repeat, taking the body toward the left.

SEQUENCE:
4 times: right, left, right, left.

In either of the preparations, the lift on count 12 can be taken into a relevé to heighten the energy for the drop on count 1.

ELEMENTARY

The elementary version is the same as the second preparation, with a change in the position of the feet on counts 10 11 12.

Count 1: Drop into second position plié, body over forward, arms down.

Count 2: Rebound.

Count 3: Use the rebound to bring the spine successively up to vertical and lift the arms successively up to the sides.

Counts 4 5 6: Plié, arching in the upper body.

Counts 7 8: Lift from the chest to straighten the legs and take the weight onto the right leg. Rotate the hips and the shoulders to the right, stretching the left leg behind you. As the body rotates, allow the lift in the chest to release the left foot off the floor. Stretch the left arm forward and the right arm out to the side.

Count 9: Keeping the left leg and the torso in one long, smooth line, allow the leg to lift behind you as a result of the tilt in the body, just as in the second preparation. Try to keep the leg in line with the body, parallel to the floor, and stretch.

Count 10: Rotate the left hip as the body swings forward, and bring the legs together into first position (Illus. 5).

Counts 11 12: Rebound and lift to bring the body up to vertical and straighten the legs. Use the lift to take you into relevé in first position. The relevé should be so lifted that the right leg can release and open into second position on the "&" count of 12. The hips should remain centered.

SEQUENCE:
Preparation #1: right, left;
Preparation #2: right, left;
Elementary version: right, left, right, left.

The goal, as you repeat the exercise, is to practice centering the weight evenly between both legs by trying to make the hip rotation and the fall and rebound in the body on counts 11 and 12 happen almost simultaneously.

EXERCISE 15
Illustration 5

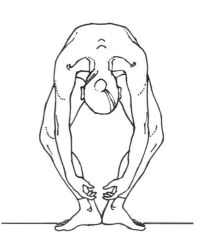

INTERMEDIATE

Before accomplishing the intermediate version, do the first preparation, right and left, and the second preparation, right and left.

Counts 1 through 9: Same as the elementary version.

Count 10: Rotate the left hip as the body swings forward. As you bring the legs together, instead of closing into a first position plié, bring the left foot into a coupé position (toes to the ankle) and plié on the right leg (Illus. 6). Keep the weight evenly distributed between both legs and be sure to keep both legs turned out.

Counts 11 12: Use the rebound in the body to start the successional roll up of the spine. Use the lift in the spine to straighten the standing leg and to bring the left leg into passé (toes to the knee); continue the lift into relevé (Illus. 7). By keeping the momentum of the fall and rebound going, you will keep yourself on balance and suspended—like a gyroscope. Open the arms as you straighten the leg and go into relevé.

Count &: On the & of count 12, open the left foot to the side into second position. As you open into second, maintain the suspension of the relevé until you fall on count 1.

Repeat to the left.

SEQUENCE:
Preparation #1: right, left;
Preparation #2: right, left; then
Intermediate version: right, left, right, left.

Throughout the exercise be aware of the central axis stretching upward as your body falls on count 10 and rebounds up to vertical on 11 and 12.

ADVANCED

The advanced version is the same as the intermediate, with the addition of a full turn on counts 10 11 12.

In order to accomplish the turn, allow the momentum of the body fall, and the rotation of the hip as it turns back out, to take the body into a full turn toward the rotating hip. Simultaneously, the spine successionally comes up to vertical and the arms lift and open successionally out to the sides.

EXERCISE 15
Illustration 6

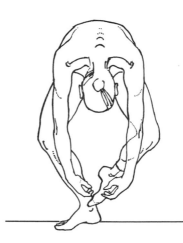

SEQUENCE:
Preparation #1: right, left;
Preparation #2: right, left;
Intermediate version: right, left; then
Body rotates right, full turn toward the left,
Body rotates left, full turn toward the right.
Repeat right and left.

NOTES TO TEACHERS

This is a very difficult exercise because students cannot rely on strength alone to carry them through the turn. This exercise calls upon all the techniques learned throughout the preceding series of exercises:

Oppositions: The oppositional pulls are working at all times to help keep the body lifted and balanced.

Successional lifts: The successional lift in the spine has a high point in the center of the back that keeps moving up the spine as the body comes up to vertical. It is the lift from that point, as the energy goes up the spine, that straightens the leg and takes the body into relevé. This is what allows the standing leg to "hang" below the hips—a feeling of the body being suspended from the high point at the top of head. The suspension is essential to balance, as it enables the leg to be stretched but not gripped or tensed.

The successional lift in the arms is a process of constant motion; the arms never stop in any position. The arms should feel as if they are moving from the center of the back. They lift and open successionally out to the sides as a result of the lift in the spine.

Fall: The potential energy in the lateral stretch (the tabletop) should be as great as that in the vertical stretch of a high relevé. Even though there is less of a distance to fall from the lateral stretch, the momentum of the fall should be great enough to create a rebound at the bottom of the fall, just as in a fall from a high relevé. In the fall from the lateral stretch, stress the use of the oppositional pull from the head to the foot to draw the head and the foot together so that they come to center at the same time, with equal force. This helps to recenter the body and will create a strong rebound.

Alignment: As the body comes up successionally in the turn, the shoulders should be aligned over the hips. This will help the body stay on balance.

Quality: It is the quality of the movement that will carry students through the exercise: the fall and rebound, the lift from the rebound, and the transformation of potential energy into kinetic energy. All these, combined with the student's own confidence that his or her body knows where to go, will create the flow and seemingly effortless character of the movement. If students find that they are a bit off center, have them work on allowing the momentum of the movement carry them through and realign them.

Labanotation for Preparation #1, Preparation #2, Intermediate and Advanced versions of this exercise is provided on page 202.

The metronome setting for this exercise is ♩ = 112.
Phrasing for musical accompaniment:

EXERCISE 15
Illustration 7

1 2 3 / 4 5 6 / 7 8 9 / 10 11 12

SIXTEEN: DROPS IN THREES

PURPOSE: To recenter and to recall the use of weight in the drop and lift.

We always did these just before going across the floor, to get back the sense of weight in the body.

METER: 3/4
TEMPO: medium

PHRASING: 1 2 3 / 2 2 3 / 3 2 3 / 4 2 3

EXERCISE 16
Illustrations 1–2

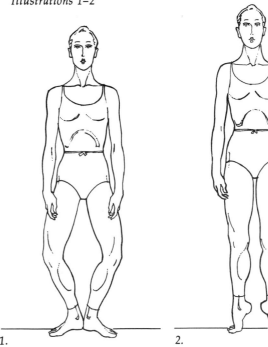

1.   2.

OPENING POSITION: First position high relevé, arms down at the sides.

PREPARATION (ALL LEVELS): This exercise will call on all the work you have done up to this point on drop and rebound, lifting in the body to relevé, and hip and shoulder alignment.

Count 1: From the high relevé, drop into first position plié, keeping the body vertical. Be sure to keep the heels on the floor as you plié (Illus. 1). Arrive in the plié by count 1. This means you will have to start the drop count 1.

Counts 2 3: Beginning at the top of the head, lift into relevé (Illus. 2). Take the full 2 counts to lift so that you do not arrive until count 3. Continue lifting in the relevé through count 3.

Repeat this several times until you are comfortable with it.

ELEMENTARY

The elementary version is the same as the preparation, with the addition of successional arms.

Count 1: Beginning in the opening position but with the arms lifted diagonally out to the sides, drop into plié. The arms drop and cross at the wrists in front of you (Illus. 3).

Counts 2 3: Take the full 2 counts to lift into relevé. Simultaneously bring the arms successively up and open them out to the sides.

Repeat this 3 times. The fourth time, as you reach the high relevé on count 3, allow the right foot to release, open to the side and suspend, so that the next drop on count 1 will be in second position.

Repeat the exercise 3 times in second position. The fourth time, as you reach the high relevé, allow the right foot to release and suspend, closing back into first position for the next drop on the count of 1.

Repeat the entire exercise, opening with the left foot.

SEQUENCE:
Preparation, then
4 times in first position with arms,
    open right foot to second;
4 times in second position with arms,
    close right foot to first.
Repeat, opening and closing with left foot.

Be sure to use both counts 2 and 3 to lift into relevé, moving the body and the arms simultaneously. Make sure that it is the fall and lift in the body that is leading the movement, rather than the arms.

EXERCISE 16
Illustrations 3–4

3.   4.

INTERMEDIATE

The intermediate version adds the upper body to the legs and arms. As you add the body, start by taking the head, shoulders and chest over forward. As you master the exercise, add the waist.

Count 1: Beginning in the opening position, arms opened up to the sides, drop into plié and drop the arms and let the upper body fall over forward (Illus. 4). Rebound in the legs and in the body to begin the relevé.

Counts 2 3: Lift to relevé, bringing the arms up and opening them out successionally as the spine rolls up to vertical. Be sure to take the full 2 counts to accomplish this.

SEQUENCE:
Preparation, then
4 times in first position with arms and body,
    open with right foot;
4 times in second position with arms and body,
    close with right foot.
Repeat, opening and closing with left foot.

Be sure that the rebound in the body and in the legs happens on count 1. The body and arm movements should be familiar to you by now.

ADVANCED

A turn is added in the advanced version. You may, if you wish, do the intermediate version once all the way through, right and left, as a preparation. The arms and body will be the same in the advanced version.

Count 1: Begin in opening position, arms open to the sides. Drop into plié and drop the arms down. The body falls over forward. Rebound in the body and in the legs to begin the relevé.

Counts 2 3: As the spine rolls up to vertical and lifts into relevé and the arms come up, use the rebound to take a full turn to the right. The weight stays on the left foot and the right foot flexes. You will need very little momentum to begin the turn; just add a little extra vertical energy on the right side, without distorting the hip and shoulder alignment. The advanced version does not open into second position.

SEQUENCE:
Optional preparation: intermediate version once through.
Once with arms, no body, no turn,
Once with arms and body, full turn to the right;
Once with arms, no body, no turn,
Once with arms and body, full turn to the left.
Repeat entire sequence, omitting preparation.

ADVANCED VARIATIONS

First Variation: This variation can be done as the first across-the-floor exercise. Step forward onto the right foot and plié on count 1, and developpé the left leg to the front as you relevé on the right (standing) leg on counts 2 and 3. Then step forward into plié on the left as you developpé the right leg to the front, and so forth across the floor, arms down at the sides throughout.

Second Variation: The across-the-floor version can be done traveling backward. It can also be done traveling sideways by crossing in front and stepping into plié on the right leg on count 1 and taking the developpé to the side with the left leg on counts 2 and 3; then stepping to the side with the left leg and taking the developpé, always crossing in front.

Third Variation: To either of the above variations can be added any combination of the body bends and successional arms. It is best, when adding body and arms, to take one set of 3 counts (step, lift, lift) without the body and arms and add them on every other step.

NOTES TO TEACHERS

The tendency of most students is to reach the high relevé on count 2, finishing the arms on count 3. Stress the simultaneous action of the arms and the body and the use of the full 2 counts to reach the high relevé.

Draw the students' attention to the rebound in the legs from the drop into plié and the use of the rebound to facilitate the relevé.

In the variations, it is important to keep the head, shoulders and hips aligned over the standing leg on each step and to keep the whole body traveling forward. This will help with balance when the body and arms are added.

Labanotation for the Intermediate and Advanced versions of this exercise are provided on page 203.

The metronome setting for this exercise is ♩ = 120.
Phrasing for musical accompaniment:

1 2 3 / 2 2 3 / 3 2 3 / 4 2 3

EXERCISE 17
Illustration 1

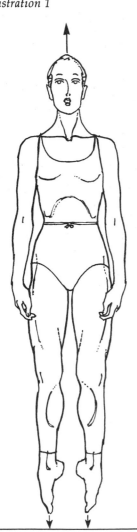

SEVENTEEN: JUMPS

PURPOSE: To increase the level of energy in preparation for across-the-floor work.

These jumps are not an essential part of the Limón technique. They appear in this part of the class in order to help build your energy.

METER: 3/8
TEMPO: fast

PHRASING: 3 / $\overset{>}{1}$ 2 3 / $\overset{>}{2}$ 2 3 / $\overset{>}{3}$ 2 3 / $\overset{>}{4}$ 2 3

OPENING POSITION: First position, arms down at the sides.

ALL LEVELS

Lift with the whole body to accomplish the jumps, instead of pushing up with the legs. Be sure to maintain the hip and shoulder alignment and to move the torso as a unit. As you straighten your legs in the jump, point your toes straight down. The arms stay down at your sides throughout the exercise. The accent is "down" on the count of 1 and "up" on counts 2 3. To get the rhythm going, take a preparatory plié and jump on count 3, landing on count 1 to jump again on counts 2 3, and so forth.

Count 1: Plié in first position.

Counts – 2 3: Use the rebound in the legs and the lift in the body to jump. Stretch your legs and feet beneath you (Illus. 1).

Count 2: Plié in first position.

Counts – 2 3: Jump.

Continue as above for 8 measures, ending in first position plié on count 8. Lift to straighten the legs and open the right leg to second position on – 2 3.

Count 1: Plié in second position.

Counts 2 3: Use the rebound in the legs and the lift in the body to jump. Stretch your legs and feet beneath you.

Count 2: Plié in second position.

Counts 2 3: Jump.

Continue as above for 8 measures, ending in second position plié on count 8. Lift to straighten the legs and close the right foot into first position. Repeat the 8 jumps in first, open the left leg to second, repeat the 8 jumps in second, close the left leg to first.

SEQUENCE:
8 jumps in first, open right leg to second,
8 jumps in second, close right leg to first,
8 jumps in first, open left leg to second,
8 jumps in second, close left leg to first.

VARIATION

Try changing the meter from 3/8 to 4/4. This will change the phrasing and the accent. Instead of 3 counts to each measure with 1 jump to each measure, there will be 4 counts to each measure, with a jump on each count. This variation uses the & counts, so that the accent is "up" on the count and "down" on the &.

METER: 4/4
PHRASING: & / 1 & 2 & 3 & 4 & /

Begin in plié on the & count and jump on the beat.

SEQUENCE:
8 jumps in first, open right leg to second,
8 jumps in second, close right leg to first,
8 jumps in first, open left leg to second,
8 jumps in second, close left leg to first.

NOTES TO TEACHERS

Have students try for a sense of suspension at the height of the jump. Labanotation for this exercise is provided on page 203.

The metronome setting for this exercise is $\quad = 112$. The metronome setting for the variation is $\quad = 104$ to 88. (The variation jumps should be done at the fast tempo (104) as a warm-up; or at the slower tempo if you are working specifically on elevation or phrasing.)

Phrasing for musical accompaniment:

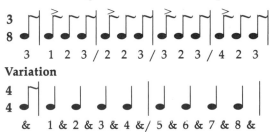

3
8
3 1 2 3 / 2 2 3 / 3 2 3 / 4 2 3

Variation

4
4
& 1 & 2 & 3 & 4 &/ 5 & 6 & 7 & 8 &

*José Limón teaching class
at the Juilliard School of Music.*

Across the Floor

EIGHTEEN: THE BODY AS AN ORCHESTRA

Across-the-floor work was always the most exciting part of José's classes. He developed a series of exercises that travel across the floor in order to coordinate in a whole dance movement all the isolated body, arm and leg movements learned in the preceding exercises.

He used the metaphor of the body as an orchestra to describe how the parts of the body relate to each other in movement. Each part of the body functions as an instrument in the orchestra, with its own special sound, or quality. The exercises teach you how to play each instrument in isolation: how each part of the body can move, how it "sounds." As you move across the floor, you will learn how the instruments harmonize, how all the parts of the body work together, to create a symphony: the music of dance movement.

The following exercise is one of many that José developed in order to teach the principle of the body as an orchestra. I have chosen to present this particular one first because it is the simplest and most straightforward.

METER: 6/4
TEMPO: medium

PHRASING: 1 2 3 4 5 6

OPENING POSITION: Standing, legs parallel, arms down at the sides.

PREPARATION (ALL LEVELS): The preparation sets up an ostinato rhythm (an unvarying rhythmic pattern) in the feet. This rhythm will remain constant throughout the exercise.

Count 1: Step forward into plié on the right leg (Illus. 1).

Count 2: Step forward onto relevé on the left leg (piqué) (Illus. 2). Feel a brief moment of suspension here—a feeling of breath.

Count 3: Without moving forward, turn the right leg out and step into plié. Place the foot directly to the side, without taking the whole body to the right (Illus. 3). At the same time bend the left leg.

Count 4: Keeping the right leg in plié, turn the left leg out and step into plié. Place the foot directly to the left side without moving the whole

EXERCISE 18
Illustrations 1–6

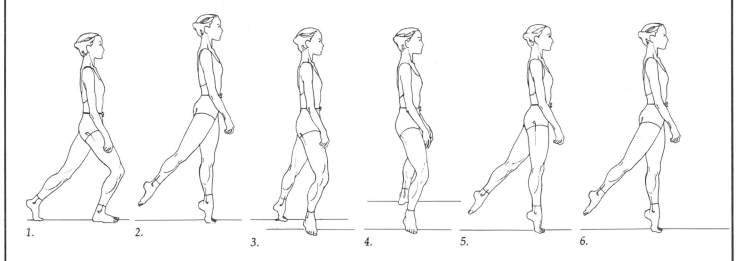

1.   2.   3.   4.   5.   6.

body to the side (Illus. 4). You should finish in a wide second-position plié.

Count 5: Turn the right leg parallel and step forward onto relevé (piqué). Step directly ahead (Illus. 5).

Count 6: Turn the left leg parallel and step forward onto relevé (piqué), stepping directly ahead (Illus. 6).

Repeat the foot pattern, traveling straight across the floor. The arms stay down at your sides and your focus should be front. Look where you are going and go there purposefully. (If you are working in a small studio, travel across the floor on the diagonal.)

Repeat the foot pattern, coming back across the floor, starting with your left foot.

This rhythm—an even 6-count rhythm—is the tympani part of the orchestra.

Foot Pattern:
1: Right leg parallel, step forward onto plié.
2: Left leg parallel, step forward onto relevé.
3: Right leg turned out, step to side in plié.
4: Left leg turned out, step to side in plié.
5: Right leg parallel, step forward onto relevé.
6: Left leg parallel, step forward onto relevé.

ELEMENTARY

The second instrument is added in the elementary version: the arms. The arms should have the quality of violins—a light, sustained quality that contrasts with the constant pulse in the legs.

The foot pattern keeps going exactly as in the preparation and the arms are added on top. When you begin the foot pattern on the right leg, begin the arm movement with the right arm.

Though the shapes of the arms are described count by count below, the movement should be a constant flow, moving as if one arm causes the other arm to move. The arms do not arrive in a shape abruptly on the count; they use the entire count to reach and pass through the shape. In order to accomplish this quality, try to think of the peak of each arm movement occurring as the arm reaches and passes through the shape. Then move the arms as if the left arm were "taking over" the peak of the movement in the right arm. As the left arm reaches and passes through the shape, it is almost as if it were trying to "top" the right arm, lifting just a shade higher.

EXERCISE 18
Illustrations 7–12

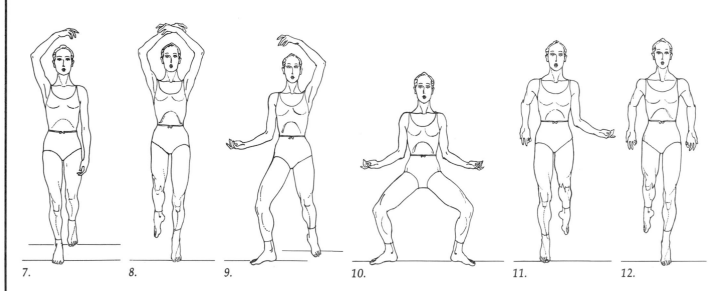

7.   8.   9.   10.   11.   12.

Count 1: Lift the right arm overhead, bent at the elbow, so that the lower arm crosses over your head, as in successional arms (Illus. 7).

Count 2: Keeping the right arm overhead, bring the left arm up in the same way, so that the lower arm crosses over your head (Illus. 8).

Count 3: Bring the right arm down toward your right side, leading with the elbow and letting the lower arm follow, palm up. The elbow should not quite touch your right side (Illus. 9).

Count 4: Bring the left arm down toward your left side in the same way, leading with the elbow and letting the lower arm follow (Illus. 10).

Count 5: Maintaining the shape of the arm, bring the right elbow back behind you (Illus. 11).

Count 6: Bring the left elbow down and back in the same way (Illus. 12). In this position you should feel as if the elbows are pulling back against the forward movement in the body.

Repeat the exercise until the coordination between the arms and the legs feels comfortable. Find the contrasts in the quality: the smooth, gliding motion in the arms juxtaposed with the more percussive, crisp movement in the legs.

INTERMEDIATE

In the intermediate version a third instrument, the body, is added. The quality of the movement in the body is that of a bassoon: weighted, yet continuous. Apply the principles of succession in the body and the arms to keep both moving fluidly.

EXERCISE 18
Illustrations 13–18

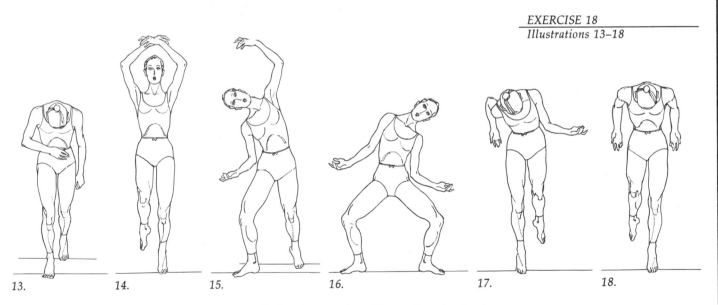

13.   14.   15.   16.   17.   18.

In the opening position, legs parallel, arms at the sides, take the body (head, shoulders, chest and waist) over forward.

Count 1: As you step forward and plié on the right leg, the body goes over forward just a bit more (Illus. 13). The right arm begins to lift.

Count 2: The body comes up successionally to vertical and the left arm begins to lift as you step onto relevé on the left leg (Illus. 14).

Count 3: Leading with the top of the head, the body goes over to the right in a side bend as you step to the right side into plié. The right arm begins to lower, elbow toward the right side. Remember to keep the stretch going through the vertical axis, lifting in the ribcage. The focus remains front (Illus. 15).

Count 4: Roll the spine successively up through vertical, keep the body going over to the left in a side bend, and bring the left arm down, elbow toward the left side. Keep the focus front (Illus. 16).

Counts 5 6: On count 5 roll the upper body forward and draw the right elbow back (Illus. 17), then draw the left elbow back on count 6 (Illus. 18), ready to begin again.

Repeat the pattern across the floor, beginning with the right foot. As you come back across the floor, begin with the left foot.

SEQUENCE:
Once through the preparation, then
4 times across the floor, beginning right, left, right, left.

As you move the upper body, remember to keep stretching through the vertical axis.

ADVANCED

The advanced version simply changes the facings. This time it is not a new instrument that is being added, but a kind of musical ornament, like a trill or arpeggio.

The movements in the legs, arms and body all remain exactly the same as in the intermediate version.

Count 1: Step forward and plié with the right foot, body over; right arm begins to lift.

Count 2: Step forward onto relevé with the left foot and take a quarter turn to the right. Turn both legs out as you do so. As the body comes successively up to vertical, the left arm begins to lift.

Count 3: Step to the right into plié, maintaining the facing. Take a side bend to the right as you bring the right arm down.

Count 4: Step to the left into plié, without changing your facing, and lift the body through vertical and over to the left side, bringing the left arm down.

Counts 5 6: Cross your right leg behind you and step onto relevé in the direction you were traveling. Bring your hips around with you and roll the body forward to bring your shoulders around and draw the right elbow, then the left elbow, back. (You will actually be making a three-quarter turn toward the right.) Step onto relevé with the left leg.

Continue across the floor. Repeat the pattern beginning with the left foot as you come back across the floor. This time the quarter turn and the three-quarter turn will be toward the left.

NOTES TO TEACHERS

This exercise should travel in a straight path across the floor, rather than on the diagonal, so that the reference points—front, side and back—are kept well defined. Two or three students can go at the same time.

Stress the lift through the vertical axis throughout the exercise. Have students concentrate on using the oppositional pulls to keep the upper body lifted and light, without losing the heaviness and weight in the legs. This will create the quality of freedom in the body along with a sense of connection to the ground.

The movement should flow continuously, with a brief stop during the moment of suspension on count 2.

In the advanced version, the tempo can be picked up in order to help blend the movements together. This will create a rebound in the first side bend. Have students use the rebound to get the body to pass through vertical and quickly over to the other side.

The aim of this exercise is to combine movements and movement qualities to create a synchronous whole, a whole that is actually more than the sum of its parts. Ideally, the movement should be so finely blended that the observer should not be able to isolate individual movements or tell if one movement is causing another.

Labanotation for this exercise is provided on page 204.

The metronome setting for this exercise is ♩=108.

Phrasing for musical accompaniment:

1 2 3 4 5 6

NINETEEN: HOP SERIES

This is one of José's exercises that we repeated in class after class as a way of discovering how to coordinate different body parts and how to change meters in a traveling combination. As in the previous across-the-floor exercise, the goal is to try to keep the feeling of weight and groundedness in the legs, while achieving the quality of lightness and sustainment in the upper body.

METER: 4/4 and 5/4
TEMPO: fast

PHRASING: $\overline{1\ 2\ 3\ 4}$ / $\overline{5\ 6\ 7\ 8}$ / $\overline{1\ 2\ 3\ 4\ 5}$

OPENING POSITION: Stand in first position, arms down.

PREPARATION (ALL LEVELS): This is for the 5-count transition between phrases. The "hops" in this exercise are not light, bobbing hops. They are more like "chugs," in which the foot barely comes off the floor and the feeling is one of heaviness in the legs. Imagine there is a glass filled with wine on the top of your head and that you do not want to spill a drop of it as you hop.

Count 1: Step onto the ball of the left foot, heel raised and pushed forward. (Take the step almost as a slide: the ball of the foot just skims the floor before you step onto it. The idea is to avoid picking up your foot and setting it down.) Extend the right leg behind you, toes pointed and leg turned out (Illus. 1). As you step onto the left foot, turn the right shoulder in toward your chest.

Counts 2 3: Hop forward twice on the ball of

EXERCISE 19
Illustration 1

the foot, keeping the right leg extended behind you. Take both counts to bring the right arm across your body in front of you, extending it successionally from the shoulder toward the left: shoulder, elbow, wrist and hand (Illus. 2).

Counts 4 5: Step forward onto the right foot on count 4. (Again, just skim the floor with the ball of the foot before stepping onto it.) Extending the left leg behind you, toes pointed and leg turned out, hop once on the right foot, landing on count 5. The action in the legs in the hop should be almost like a split in the air. At the same time, open the right shoulder and take both counts to successionally extend the right arm to the side, beginning at the shoulder.

As you do this transition, imagine that you are drawing a curtain across in front of you during counts 1 2 3. On counts 4 and 5, you open the curtain and hop in front of it. This should help to give you the sense of moving forward, rather than up, on the last hop.

ELEMENTARY

This is the 8-count phrase which occurs before the 5-count transition you just practiced in the Preparation. When you put them together, the exercise will be: 8-count phrase, 5-count transition twice (the transition alternates feet), 8-count phrase, 5-count transition twice, and so forth.

Counts 1 2: Starting from the opening position, step onto the ball of the right foot, extending the left leg behind you (just as in the Preparation), and curve both arms toward the right—the left arm across the front of the body—palms up (Illus. 3, solid lines) on count 1. Hop on count 2.

Counts 3 4: Continue hopping on the right foot, once on count 3 and once on count 4. Take both counts to bring the arms overhead, elbows pulled back slightly, palms facing forward (Illus. 3).

Counts 5 6: Continue hopping on the right foot, once on count 5 and once on count 6. Take both counts to bring the arms down toward the left side, leading with the fingertips, elbows lifted, palms down (Illus. 3). The shoulders rotate as the arms go down in order to accommodate the lifting of the elbows.

Counts 7 8: Drop the body over forward and step into plié on the left foot, then step into plié on the right foot, moving forward. The arms come down to your sides. These two steps should be weighty.

EXERCISE 19
Illustration 2

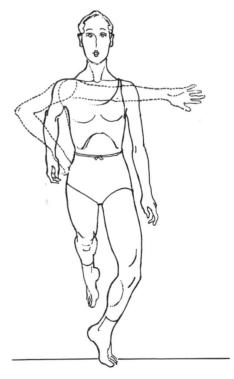

You are now ready to step onto the left foot for the hops in the transition. Do the 5-count transition twice and continue alternating the 8-count phrase with two 5-count transitions as you travel across the floor.

INTERMEDIATE

The 8-count phrase in the intermediate version is the same as the elementary version with the addition of the body throughout the phrase and a turn on counts 7 8. Because of the turn, which does not change feet, the transition phrase starts on the right foot. Other than that, the 5-count transition phrase for the intermediate version is identical to the Preparation.

Counts 1 2: Step forward onto the ball of the right foot, extending the left leg behind you, and curve the arms toward the right, left arm across the body. Take the body into a side bend toward the right, palms up (Illus. 4, solid lines). Hop on count 2.

Counts 3 4: Continue hopping on the right foot and take the upper back into an arch as you bring the arms overhead (Illus. 4).

Counts 5 6: Continue hopping on the right foot and take the body into a side bend to the left as you bring the arms down to the left (Illus. 4).

Counts 7 8: Step forward into plié on the left foot, swing the body forward from the side bend, and rebound, using the momentum of the body swing and the rebound to take a full turn toward the right. Use a successional roll up in the spine to straighten the legs and take you into relevé as you complete the turn. As you turn, keep the right leg extended slightly off the floor and turned out, so that it finishes in front of you. The arms come down to the sides during the turn.

Continue across the floor, alternating the 8-count phrase with two 5-count transition phrases.

ADVANCED

This is exactly the same as the intermediate version, with the first 6 counts changed to a turn in place. As in the intermediate version, the transition phrase will begin on the right foot since the turn on counts 7 8 does not change feet.

Counts 1 2: Step onto the ball of the right foot

EXERCISE 19
Illustration 3

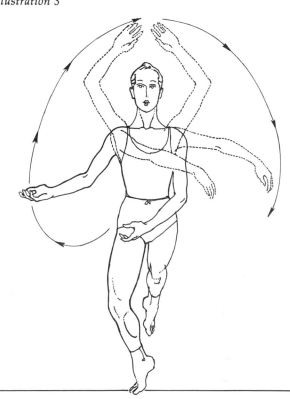

and take the body in a side bend to the right, arms curving to the right. Hop on count 2. As you step and hop on counts 1 and 2, take a quarter turn to the right (clockwise). The arms and the body lead into the turn.

Counts 3 4: Continue hopping on the right foot, and take another quarter turn to the right so that you are facing back. Simultaneously, take the upper body into an arch and bring the arms overhead.

Counts 5 6: Continue hopping on the right foot, and this time take a quarter turn to the right on each hop so that you end facing front. Take the body into a side bend to the left and bring the arms down to the left side, leading with the fingertips.

Counts 7 8: Step forward onto the left foot, swing the body forward from the side bend and rebound, using the momentum of the body swing and the rebound to take a full turn toward the right. Use the successional roll up in the spine to straighten the legs and take you into relevé as you complete the turn. Keep the right leg extended in front of you, slightly off the floor, during the turn so that it ends in front of you. The arms come down to the sides during the turn.

Do the 5-count transition phrase twice and continue alternating the 8-count phrase and two 5-count transitions as you travel across the floor.

ADVANCED VARIATIONS

Variations on the 8-count phrase: Keep traveling forward across the floor as you take the turn on the first six counts of the advanced version.

Variation on the 5-count phrase: As you do the transition phrase, turn in place toward the working leg (if you are hopping on the right leg, turn toward the right). Use the shoulder as the impetus for the turn.

The quality of this movement should be one of continual motion, and all the parts of the body (or all the instruments of the orchestra) should be in harmony. It takes more than just the technical points I have outlined in this book to make this movement really sing. The technique will put all the parts in the right place, doing the right thing at the right time; the accents and phrasing will create the dynamics; but it is the ability of each individual

EXERCISE 19
Illustration 4

dancer to project the qualities of the movement that transforms it from exercise into performance.

NOTES TO TEACHERS

Another variation on the advanced version is to speed up the tempo and change the exercise to a 6-count phrase with two 5-count transitions. Have students eliminate the hopping on counts 1 through 6 and accomplish them as a smooth, continuous turn in place in counts 1 2 3. The turn that was originally on counts 7 and 8 remains the same, with the counts changing to 4 5 6. Then, in the first of the two 5-count transitions, have students eliminate the hops on the first 3 counts and accomplish them as a turn in place. Keep the hop forward on counts 4 and 5. The second of the 5-count transitions stays the same, with all the hops, so that the exercise will travel across the floor.

This variation is counted as follows:

Phrase:
1 2 3: Turn on right foot toward right.
4 5 6: Step onto left foot, turn toward right.

Transition:
1 2 3: Step onto right foot, turn toward right.
4 5: Step onto left foot, hop forward.
1 2 3: Step onto right foot, hop forward twice.
4 5: Step onto left foot, hop forward.

The body swing and rebound provide the momentum for the turns.
Labanotation for this exercise and variations is provided on page 204.

The metronome setting for this exercise is ♩ = 152.
Phrasing for musical accompaniment:

TWENTY: PIQUÉ SERIES

José taught this exercise in the first class I ever had with him. I have added two variations to the version he taught, which appear at the end of this exercise.

METER: 4/4
TEMPO: elementary and intermediate: slow
advanced: fast
PHRASING: 1 2 3 4

OPENING POSITION: Standing in first position, arms down at the sides. This exercise is best done straight forward, toward the mirror or the front of the room, rather than across the studio as in the two previous exercises.

ELEMENTARY

Count 1: With the right foot, take a forward step across toward the left. Step onto the ball of the foot with a straight leg (piqué). Simultaneously, bring the left leg to passé, keeping the leg turned out and placing the toes slightly behind the right knee; and scoop the right arm out from the side and up, leading with the palm of the hand and curving the arm. Be sure to lift from the high point in the top of the head.

Count 2: Suspend the lift in the body and keep the arm moving until it is directly overhead. Bring the toes of the left foot to the front of the right knee by lifting the left knee to move the toes. This is a moment in which you can practice using the lift in the high point to extend the movement and to feel the suspension (Illus. 1, solid lines).

EXERCISE 20
Illustration 1

Counts 3 4: Cross the left foot in front and step into plié. At the same time, circle the right arm down in front (Illus. 1, dotted lines). Step out to the right side into plié on the right foot and continue the circle of the arm down and to the right side.

Repeat by stepping across with the left foot onto piqué and bringing the right leg to passé. Continue forward, alternating starting legs and arms.

SEQUENCE:
Right, left, right, left,
traveling toward the front of the room.

The most important thing to work for in this exercise is the suspension on count 2. You want to create the quality of suspension not only in the body but also in the lift of the arm and the passé leg.

INTERMEDIATE

EXERCISE 20
Illustration 2

This version has the same foot and arm pattern as the elementary version, with the addition of a side bend in the body. The opening position is also slightly different: Start standing in first position plié with the arms down to the sides and the upper body in a side bend to the right.

Count 1: With the right leg, step across toward the left onto piqué and start to successively lift the upper body to vertical while scooping the right arm out and up. Neither the body nor the arm reach their full height on the count of 1.

Count 2: As you lift in the suspension, bring the right arm overhead and continue the body up through vertical, then start the body in an arc into a side bend to the left (Illus. 2, solid lines).

Counts 3 4: Step across with the left foot into plié and continue to deepen the side bend to the left, taking it into the waist (Illus. 2, dotted lines). At the same time, circle the right arm down in front. Then, with the right leg step out to the right side into plié, and continue to deepen the side bend and lift in the high point, which will be in the ribcage on the right side. Bring the right arm down to the side. You are now ready to repeat the sequence, this time leading with the left foot and circling the left arm, with the body in a wide bend to the left in the opening position.

SEQUENCE:
Right, left, right, left,
traveling toward the front of the room.

Slow down the speed of the body slightly to accommodate the suspension. This is actually a traveling suspension, in which the upper body goes through vertical before it begins the side bend to the other side.

ADVANCED

In the advanced version counts 1 and 2 become a jump that uses the lift in the body, the arm and the passé knee to take you into the air. The opening position is the same as the intermediate opening position.

Counts 1 and 2: Step across in front with the right leg into plié. Use the lift of the body rolling up to vertical, the lift of the right arm scooping up overhead and the lift in the left knee as it comes into passé to take you into a jump. Suspend the jump on count 2.

Counts 3 4: Come down into plié on the right leg, continuing the arc in the upper body into the side bend to the left, and circle the right arm down in front. With the left leg step out to the right side into plié, deepening the side bend and bringing the arm down to your side.

Move immediately into the lift and jump of the next counts 1 and 2.

SEQUENCE:
Right, left, right, left,
traveling toward the front of the room.

Be sure to maintain the body bend all the way through counts 3 and 4. Do not anticipate the lift in the body; wait until count 1 and use the momentum of the lift in the body to help you jump.

Try to give the jump the same quality of suspension as the piqué in the elementary and intermediate versions.

ADVANCED VARIATIONS

FIRST VARIATION: Add a turn to the intermediate version so that you will turn toward the standing leg as the body rises and goes through vertical on counts 1 and 2. You do not have to be strict with the counts on the turn. As you step onto piqué use the lift in the arm and body to start the turn. Scoop the arm slightly behind you, instead of directly to the side, and use that momentum to start the turn. Use the lift and suspension through vertical to bring you back around. You should be vertical and centered at the beginning of count 2. Take the body to the left as you complete the turn. As you alternate sides try to keep the body in the side bend until the piqué.

Challenge yourself to maintain the sense of suspension throughout the turn. It is easier to piqué, come to vertical and then turn, but this exercise is concerned with keeping the changes in the upper body flowing continuously on top of the action in the legs.

Do the intermediate version 4 times: right, left, right, left. Then do the variation with turns 4 times: right, left, right, left.

SECOND VARIATION (FOR ADVANCED AND PROFESSIONAL DANCERS ONLY): Add a jump to the turn in variation #1. Be absolutely sure that the standing leg in the jump stays turned out as you turn. If you allow it to turn parallel or to turn in, you will put a strain on the ankle as you land.

Do the advanced version 4 times (right, left, right, left), do the first variation 4 times, and then do the second variation 4 times.

Labanotation for the Intermediate and Advanced versions and for the variations of this exercise is provided on page 205.

The metronome setting for this exercise is ♩ = 112 for elementary and intermediate levels, ♩ = 144 for advanced.

Phrasing for musical accompaniment:

Ending Class

At the end of class I bring my students back to the center of the floor for series of pliés. This is almost like a *révérence*, the formal ending of a ballet class, but it is done for a different reason. I do it to recenter the body after going across the floor and to take a moment to relax any tension that may have built up in the muscles.

Standing in first position, do 2 demi-pliés (plié without lifting the heels off the floor) at a slow tempo, followed by a grand plié. In the grand plié, as you go down, lift the arms slowly, leading with the elbows and keeping the arms curved out to the sides. As you come up from the plié, turn the elbows over and slowly lower the arms, palms up, leading with the elbows. Feel the opposition of the elbows lifting and the body lowering, and then the opposition of the elbows lowering and the body lifting.

Take a breath and, as in the preparatory exercise for alignment (page 37), use the breath to take the body into a high relevé. Hiss the breath out and allow the heels to lower, keeping the top of the head lifting toward the ceiling. Your body is now correctly aligned. (If it is more comfortable for you, you can turn your legs parallel as you lower the heels.)

Daniel Lewis teaching at the Juilliard School.

Then, keeping that alignment, imagine that your body is filled with sand and that the sand is slowly pouring out of your feet. Empty your legs first, starting at the ankles, and work progressively upward through the body, until the entire body is emptied. Remember to empty your neck and head, too. Let the sand in your arms pour out through your fingertips. This is intended to help relax your muscles as your skeleton remains standing tall and properly aligned.

Before I dismiss this class, let me say, "Thank you."

PETER SCHAAF

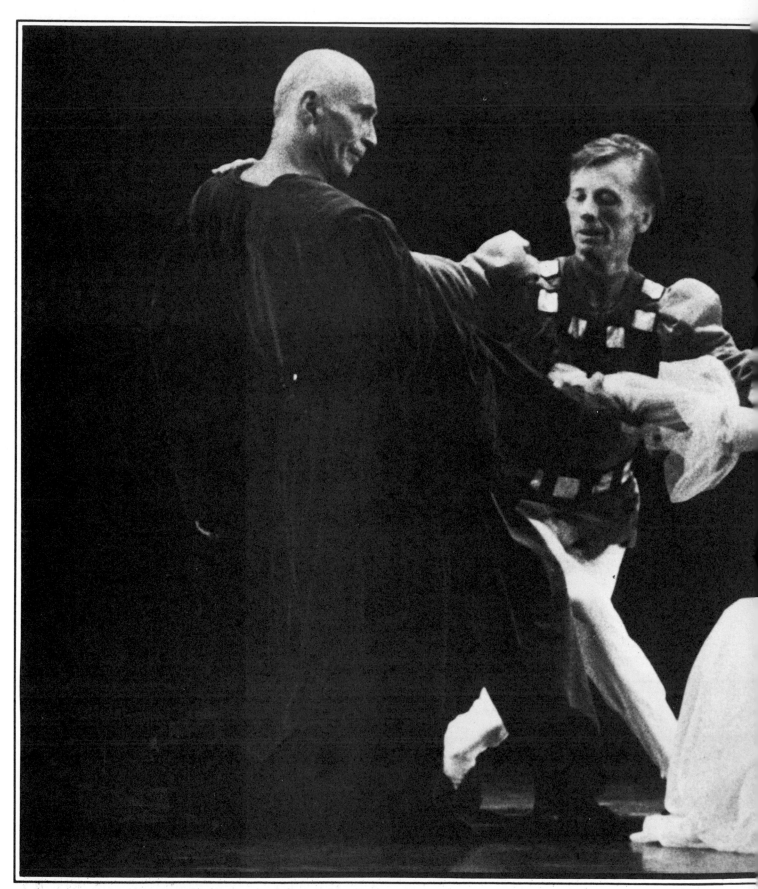

José Limón, Lucas Hoving and Betty Jones in a rehearsal of The Moor's Pavane.

PART FOUR

Repertory

*I try to compose works
that are involved
with man's basic tragedy
and the grandeur of
his spirit. I want to dig
beneath empty
formalisms, displays
of technical virtuosity,
and the slick surface; to
probe the human entity
for the powerful,
often crude, beauty of
the gesture that speaks
of man's humanity.*

JOSÉ LIMÓN, "THE MODERN
DANCE AS AN UNPOPULAR ART"

From *Missa Brevis*

A large portion of José's classes dealt with applying what we learned in the technical part of the class to selections from his choreographic repertory. At this point the qualities, the rhythm and the dynamics were carefully defined, the movement polished and perfected. This was also a time when dancers worked on projecting the movement in performance.

One of my favorite repertory phrases, both in class and on stage, is from the "Cum Sancto Spiritu" section of *Missa Brevis,* choreographed to Zoltán Kodály's music. This was the first Limón work I ever performed. José choreographed it in 1958, after a State Department tour of Europe. He wrote in a letter to a friend soon after his return: "Against a background of cities still lying eviscerated by the savagery of war, I met human beings of courage, serenity, nobility. There was no rancor, no bitterness. Only a

Illustration 2   *Illustration 1*

tremendous resolution, a sense of the future." It was this spirit of hope, the power of group unity, as well as the strength of the individual, that José tried to capture in the *Missa Brevis*.

The "Cum Sancto Spiritu" section is a quartet for four men. At the end of the section the men perform a leaping phrase in unison, to the music of a large chorus singing a series of sustained amens. The phrase travels downstage on a diagonal path. José used to lead the quartet. The power of the movement itself and José's long leaping strides seemed to pull us forward. This was the moment when I really felt the true spirit of the work.

METER: 4/4
TEMPO: medium
PHRASING: 1 2 3 4 / 5 6 7 8

OPENING POSITION: Standing legs parallel, arms down at the sides. From the left side of the room or stage, start in the farthest upstage corner, facing down on the diagonal (see the floor plan that accompanies the Labanotation on page 205).

This phrase is not broken down into elementary, intermediate and advanced levels; anyone can try it. I think the easiest way is to read it all the way through first, so that you get a picture of the progression of the movement. Then go ahead and do it.

Count 1: Step on the left foot and push off into a stag leap: leading with the right knee, leap forward on the diagonal path and keep the left leg straight behind you. As you leap, take your upper body over forward (head, shoulders, chest) and bring the arms up straight in front of you, out from your shoulders, hands flexed, fingers reaching out to the side (Illus. 1).

Count 2: Land in plié on the right foot, keeping the left leg stretched behind you. The body and the arms do not change (Illus. 2).

Count 3: Keeping the body where it is, step forward into plié on the left leg. At the same time bring the left arm down in front of you, leading with the elbow (Illus. 3, solid lines). Then straighten the arm, spreading the fingers, and allow the body to begin to come to vertical (Illus. 3, dotted lines).

Count 4: With the right leg step ahead onto relevé (Illus. 4), straighten the knee, and lift the upper body into an arch. Simultaneously, turn counterclockwise on the right leg, keeping the left leg low, straight and turned out in front of you. As you step onto the right leg into the turn, bring

Illustration 3

the right arm down in front, leading with the elbow, fingers spread, and cross both arms at the wrist at the end of the turn. The arch in the upper body occurs during the turn. You should end up facing stage front, so that you are actually doing a turn and a quarter (Illus. 5).

Count 5: Allow the left leg to continue around out of the turn and step toward the left into plié. The arms remain crossed in front and the upper body is still arched, focus up (Illus. 6, solid lines).

Count 6: Step across in front with the right leg into plié, still moving directly toward the left side of the stage (Illus. 6, dotted lines). Use this step as a take-off for a jump: another low stag leap, leading with the left knee directly sideways. You are still moving toward the left side of the stage. Keep the body arched and the arms crossed in front of you. Keep both legs turned out and both hips facing front (Illus. 7). The jump lands on Count 7.

Count 7: Land in plié on your left leg, keeping the right leg extended off the floor toward the right. Be sure both legs are turned out as you land. Allow the upper body to continue the momentum of the jump and go into a side bend to your left. The arms soften and come into a low first, swinging slightly to your left. (Illus. 8).

Count 8: With the right leg, step toward the downstage right diagonal into plié and swing the upper body and hips around to face the same diagonal. You are now ready to repeat the phrase, continuing downstage on a diagonal path.

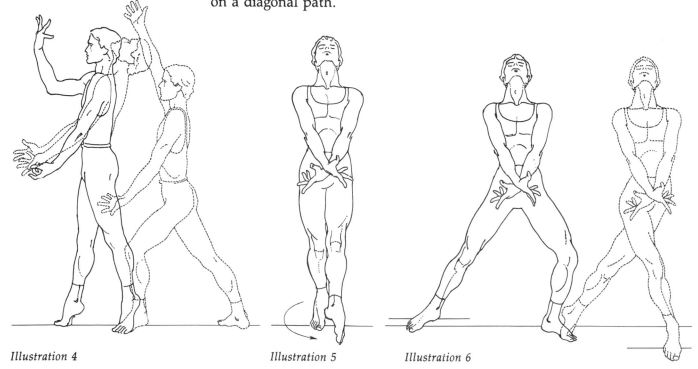

Illustration 4

Illustration 5

Illustration 6

NOTES TO TEACHERS

The sequence should never stop moving, in spite of the heavy, labored quality of the weight.

In the music, the amens overlap in a series of sustained tones, set on top of a strong metered rhythm. Encourage students to try to reflect these elements of Kodály's music by contrasting sustainment in the upper body with the driving rhythmic pattern in the legs and feet.

Do not emphasize height in either of the jumps; rather concentrate more on traveling through space. This is true for the whole phrase. The movement derives its exciting quality from the driving forward momentum and the earthy groundedness of the weight.

When teaching repertory, I tell students to forget about the technique and to let their muscle memory take over. This enables them to focus on the quality of the movement and helps them to perform it. One way to teach this is to break down the movement into the leg pattern, the arm pattern and the body pattern.

Labanotation for the "Cum Sancto Spiritu" section of *Missa Brevis* is provided on page 205.

The metronome setting for this exercise is ♩ = 100.
Phrasing for musical accompaniment:

$$\frac{4}{4}$$ ♩ ♩ ♩ ♩ | ♩ ♩ ♩ ♩ |

1 2 3 4 / 5 6 7 8

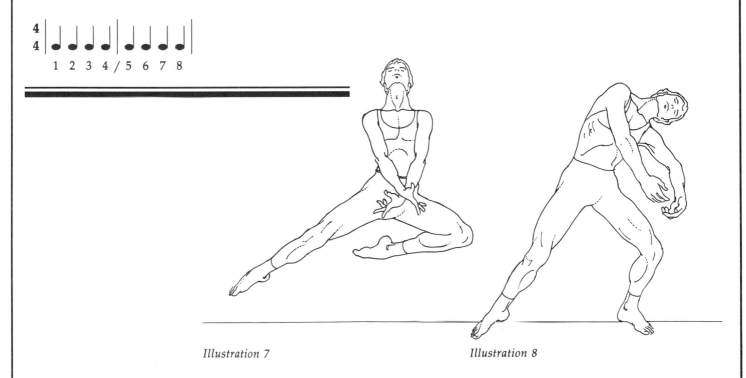

Illustration 7   Illustration 8

José Limón in A Choreographic Offering.

PART FIVE

Appendix

My first requisite is an idea. I cannot function with abstractions, or with what is called absolute dance. I work out of the emotions, out of human experience, mine or those about which I have read or heard. Certainly there has to be a deeply felt motive or subject. There is usually a period of about two years during which I live with the idea. I think about it, usually during the long train rides across the continent on our concert tours. I sleep with it, and I eat with it. I become obsessed and possessed. I try all sorts of movements and gestures which occur spontaneously, in the studio, or when I fancy that I am alone and unobserved, waiting for a subway, or an elevator, or in a room by myself....

JOSÉ LIMÓN,
"COMPOSING A DANCE"

Works Choreographed by José Limón

ALPHABETICAL LISTING BY TITLE

ANTIGONA *(Ensemble work for 8)*

Premiere:	March 1951, at the Palacio de Bellas Artes, Mexico City
Music:	*Sinfonia de Antigona* by Carlos Chavez
Costumes and Set:	Miguel Covarrubias

THE APOSTATE *(Trio)*

Premiere:	August 15, 1959, at Connecticut College American Dance Festival, New London
Music:	*Elegy for Strings* by Ernst Krenek
Costumes:	Pauline Lawrence
Set:	Ming Cho Lee

BACCHANALE *(Trio)*

Premiere:	December 1930, at the Humphrey-Weidman Studio, New York City
Music:	Percussion score

BACH SUITE *(Duet)*

Premiere:	Spring 1932, at the Humphrey-Weidman Studio, New York City
Music:	*Suite in B Minor for Flute and Orchestra* by Johann Sebastian Bach
Costumes:	Charles Weidman

BARREN SCEPTRE   *(Duel)*

Premiere: August 8, 1960, at the Juilliard Concert Hall,
New York City; choreographed in collaboration
with Pauline Koner
Music: Music for violin, piano and percussion
by Gunther Schuller
Costumes: Pauline Lawrence
Lighting: Thomas De Gaetani

BLUE ROSES   *(Ensemble work for 10)*

Premiere: August 16, 1957, at the Connecticut College
American Dance Festival, New London
Music: Orchestral score by William Loring
based on themes by Paul Bowles
Costumes: Pauline Lawrence
Lighting: Spofford Beadle

CANCIÓN Y DANZA   *(Male solo)*

Premiere: April 30, 1933, at Studio 61, Carnegie Hall,
New York City
Music: *Canción y Danza* by Federico Mompou

CARLOTA   *(Ensemble work for 9)*

Premiere: October 5, 1972, at the City Center American
Dance Marathon, ANTA Theatre, New York City
Music: This work is performed in silence
Costumes: Charles D. Tomlinson
Lighting: Chenault Spence

CHACONNE   *(Male solo)*

Premiere: December 27, 1942, at the Humphrey-Weidman
Studio Theater, New York City
Music: "Chaconne" from the *Partita #2 in D Minor
for Unaccompanied Violin*
by Johann Sebastian Bach

*Risa Steinberg and Carla
Maxwell in* Carlota.

A CHOREOGRAPHIC OFFERING   *(Ensemble work for 28)*

In Memory of Doris Humphrey

The Juilliard Dance Ensemble in A Choreographic Offering.

Premiere:	August 15, 1964, at the Connecticut College American Dance Festival, New London
Music:	*A Musical Offering* by Johann Sebastian Bach
Costumes:	Pauline Lawrence
Lighting:	Thomas Skelton

COMEDY   *(Ensemble work for 16)*

Premiere:	August 10, 1968, at the Connecticut College American Dance Festival, New London
Music:	Josef Wittman
Costumes:	Pauline Lawrence
Lighting:	Thomas Skelton

CONCERT   *(Sextet)*

Premiere:	August 19, 1950, at the Connecticut College American Dance Festival, New London
Music:	*Six Preludes and Fugues* by Johann Sebastian Bach, arranged by Simon Sadoff
Costumes:	Pauline Lawrence

CONCERTO GROSSO (Trio)

Premiere: May 19, 1945, at the Humphrey-Weidman Studio,
New York City
Music: *Concerto Grosso in D Minor*
by Antonio Vivaldi
Costumes: Pauline Lawrence

CURTAIN RAISER (Duet)

Premiere: March 1941, Seattle, Washington; choreographed
in collaboration with May O'Donnell
Music: *Theme from Suite (1930), Theme and
Variations, March from Pieces for Children*
and *American Pastorale* by Ray Green
Costumes: Claire Falkenstein

DANCES (Ensemble work for 8)

Premiere: August 15, 1958, at the Connecticut College
American Dance Festival, New London
Music: Selection of mazurkas by Frederic Chopin
Costumes: Lavina Nielsen
Lighting: Thomas Skelton

DANCES FOR ISADORA (Female quintet)

Premiere: December 16, 1971,
at the Cleveland Museum of Art,
Cleveland, Ohio
Music: Selected études and preludes
by Frederic Chopin
Costumes: Charles D. Tomlinson
Lighting: Edward Effron

DANZA (Male solo)

Premiere: April 30, 1933, at Studio 61, Carnegie Hall,
New York City
Music: *Danza* by Sergei Prokofiev

Laura Glenn
in Dances for Isadora.

DANZA   *(Male solo)*

Premiere: August 1945, Jacob's Pillow,
                Lee, Massachusetts
Music: *Danza* by J. Arcadio
Costumes: Pauline Lawrence

DANZA DE LA MUERTE   *(Quartet)*

Premiere: August 1937, Bennington College,
                Bennington, Vermont
Music: *Danza de la Muerte* by Henry Clark
                and Norman Lloyd
Costumes: Charles Weidman

DANZAS MEXICANAS   *(Male solo)*

Premiere: August 1939, Bennington-Mills,
                Oakland, California
Music: *Danzas Mexicanas* by Lionel Nowak

THE DEMON   *(Ensemble work for 7)*

Premiere: March 13, 1963, at the Juilliard Concert Hall,
                New York City
Music: Paul Hindemith
Set and
Costumes: Malcolm McCormick
Lighting: Thomas De Gaetani

DIALOGUES   *(Male duet)*

Premiere: March 1951, at the Palacio de Bellas Artes,
                Mexico City
Music: *Dialogues* by Norman Lloyd
Costumes: Julio Prieto

DON JUAN FANTASIA (Quintet)

(A Ghostly Tryst)

Premiere: August 22, 1953, at the Connecticut College
American Dance Festival, New London
Music: *Don Juan Fantasie* by Franz Liszt
Costumes: Pauline Lawrence
Lighting: Thomas Skelton

EDEN TREE (Trio)

Premiere: May 19, 1945, at the Humphrey-Weidman Studio,
New York City
Music: *Triptych* by Carl Engel
Costumes: Pauline Lawrence

EL GRITO (Ensemble work for 21)

(formerly Redes)

Premiere: First U.S. performance: December 5, 1952,
at the Juilliard School of Music, New York City
Music: *Redes*, from a film score
by Silvestre Revueltas
Costumes: Consuela Gana
Scenario: José Revueltas

THE EMPEROR JONES (Ensemble work for 8 men)

Premiere: July 12, 1956, at the Empire State Music
Festival, Ellenville, New York
Music: *The Emperor Jones* by Heitor Villa-Lobos
Costumes: Pauline Lawrence
Settings: Kim Edgar Swados

*Lucas Hoving and José Limón
in* The Emperor Jones.

ÉTUDE IN D FLAT MAJOR   *(Duet)*

Premiere:	December 1930, at the Humphrey-Weidman Studio, New York City
Music:	*Étude in D Flat Major* by Alexander Scriabin

THE EXILES   *(Duet)*

Premiere:	August 11, 1950, at the Connecticut College American Dance Festival, New London
Music:	*Chamber Symphony #2, Op. 38* by Arnold Schoenberg
Costumes:	Pauline Lawrence
Decor:	Anita Weschler

Louis Falco and Sarah Stackhouse in The Exiles.

HYMN   *(Male solo)*

Premiere:	March 15, 1936, at the Majestic Theater, New York City
Music:	Percussion played by Katherine Manning
Costumes:	José Limón

I, ODYSSEUS   *(Ensemble work for 16)*

Premiere: August 18, 1962, at the Connecticut College
                American Dance Festival, New London
Music: Hugh Aitkens
Costumes: Nellie Hatfield and Elizabeth Parsons
Properties: Thomas Watson and William McIver
Lighting: Thomas Skelton

KING'S HEART   *(Ensemble work for 9)*

Premiere: April 27, 1956, at the Juilliard School of Music,
                New York City
Music: *King's Heart* by Stanley Wolfe
Costumes: Pauline Lawrence
Set Piece: Durevol Quitzow

LA MALINCHE   *(Trio)*

Premiere: May 1947, at Jordan Hall,
                Boston, Massachusetts
Music: *La Malinche* by Norman Lloyd
Costumes: Pauline Lawrence

*Daniel Lewis
in* La Malinche.

LEGEND   *(Male trio)*

Premiere: August 17, 1968, at the Connecticut College
                  American Dance Festival, New London
Music: Tape collage of speeches and music
                  arranged by Simon Sadoff
Costumes: Pauline Lawrence
Lighting: Michael Rabbitt

*José Limón rehearsing
Legend with Clyde Morgan
and Louis Falco.*

LOS CUATROS SOLES   *(Ensemble work for 30)*

(The Four Suns)

Premiere: March 1951, at the Palacio de Bellas Artes,
                  Mexico City
Music: *Los Cuatros Soles* by Carlos Chavez
**Scenery
and
Costumes:**   Miguel Covarrubias
Story: Carlos Chavez and Miguel Covarrubias

MAC ABER'S DANCE   *(Ensemble work for 25)*

Premiere: April 20, 1967, at the Juilliard Concert Hall,
                 New York City
Music: *Animus I for Trombone and Electronic Tape*
                 by Jacob Druckman
Lighting: Sidney Bennett

MASQUERADE   *(Male solo)*

Premiere: Only performance: 1946, in St. Louis, Missouri
Music: *Sonata No. 5 in C Major, Op. 38*
                 by Sergei Prokofiev

MISSA BREVIS   *(Ensemble work for 22)*

Premiere: April 11, 1958, at the Juilliard School of Music,
                 New York City
Music: *Missa Brevis in Tempore Belli*
                 by Zoltán Kodály
**Projection
and
Costumes:**   Ming Cho Lee
Lighting: Thomas De Gaetani

*The Juilliard Dance Ensemble
in the opening of* Missa Brevis.

THE MOIRAI (Quartet)

(The Fates)

Premiere:	August 18, 1961, at the Connecticut College American Dance Festival, New London
Music:	Hugh Aitken
Costumes:	Pauline Lawrence
Lighting:	Thomas Skelton

THE MOOR'S PAVANE (Quartet)

Premiere:	August 17, 1949, at the Connecticut College American Dance Festival, New London
Music:	From various orchestral suites by Henry Purcell
Costumes:	Pauline Lawrence

José Limón directing Bruce Marks in The Moor's Pavane.

MY SON, MY ENEMY (Ensemble work for 20)

Premiere:	August 14, 1965, at the Connecticut College American Dance Festival, New London
Music:	Vivian Fine
Costumes:	Pauline Lawrence and Charles D. Tomlinson
Lighting:	Thomas Skelton

NOSTALGIC FRAGMENTS   *(Duet)*

Premiere: December 22, 1935, at the Adelphi Theater,
New York City

Music: *Suite pour Petit Orchestre, No. 2*
by Igor Stravinsky

Costumes: Charles Weidman

ODE TO THE DANCE   *(Sextet)*

Premiere: January 29, 1954, at the Juilliard School
of Music, New York City

Music: *Capricorn Concerto, Op. 21* by Samuel Barber

Set: Paul Trautvetter

Costumes: Pauline Lawrence

ORFEO   *(Quintet)*

Premiere: October 2, 1972, in the City Center American
Dance Marathon at the ANTA Theatre,
New York City

Music: *String Quartet #11, Op. 59*
by Ludwig van Beethoven

Costumes: Charles D. Tomlinson

Lighting: Chenault Spence

PERFORMANCE   *(Ensemble work for 36)*

Premiere: April 14, 1961, at the Juilliard Concert Hall,
New York City

Music: *Variations on a Theme of William Schuman*
by Hugh Aitken, William Bersgma, Jacob Druckman,
Vittorio Giannini, Norman Lloyd, Vincent
Persichetti, Robert Starer, Hugo Weisgall

Lighting: Thomas De Gaetani

PETITE SUITE   *(Trio)*

Premiere: Spring 1931, at the Humphrey-Weidman Studio,
New York City

Music: "Cortège" from *Petite Suite*
by Claude Debussy

PIÈCES FROIDES   *(Male solo)*

Premiere: April 30, 1933, at Studio 61, Carnegie Hall,
New York City
Music: *Pièces Froides* by Erik Satie

LA PIÑATA   *(Ensemble work for 31)*

Premiere: March 20, 1969, at the Juilliard Concert Hall,
New York City
Music: *La Piñata* by Burrill Phillips
Costumes: Pauline Lawrence and Betty Williams
Lighting: Sidney Bennett

PRELUDE   *(Duet)*

Premiere: December 22, 1935, at the Adelphi Theater,
New York City
Music: *Music from Aubade* by François Poulenc
Costumes: Charles Weidman

PSALM   *(Ensemble work for 16)*

Premiere: August 19, 1967, at the Connecticut College
American Dance Festival, New London
Music: *Psalm* by Eugene Lester
Costumes: Pauline Lawrence
Lighting: Thomas Skelton

THE QUEEN'S EPICEDIUM   *(Female trio)*

Premiere: August 18, 1951, at the Connecticut College
American Dance Festival, New London
Music: *Elegy on the Death of Queen Mary*
by Henry Purcell
Costumes: Pauline Lawrence

REDES (Ensemble work for 26)

Premiere: November 1951, at the Palacio de Bellas Artes, Mexico City
Music: *Redes* from a film score by Silvestre Revueltas
Costumes: Department of Theatrical Productions
Text: José Revueltas

REVEL (Ensemble work for 12)

Premiere: May 5, 1971, at the Juilliard Theater, New York City
Music: *Woodwind Quartet* by Elizabeth Sayer
Costumes: Charles D. Tomlinson
Lighting: William H. Batchelder

SATIRIC LAMENT (Duet)

Premiere: February 26, 1936, at the New School for Social Research, New York City
Music: *Music from Aubade* by François Poulenc

SCHERZO (Ensemble work for 9 men)

Premiere: May 11, 1955, at the Juilliard School of Music, New York City
Music: Percussion improvisation by John Barracuda, Stoddard Lincoln and Lucy Venable

SCHERZO (Quartet)

Premiere: August 19, 1955, at the Connecticut College American Dance Festival, New London
Music: *Scherzo* (percussion score) by Hazel Johnson

SERENATA (Quartet)

Premiere: August 14, 1958, at the Connecticut College American Dance Festival, New London
Music: Paul Bowles
Set: Thomas Watson
Lighting: Thomas Skelton

SONATA FOR TWO CELLOS   *(Solo)*

Premiere: August 19, 1961, at the Connecticut College
               American Dance Festival, New London
Music: Meyer Kupferman
Costumes: Pauline Lawrence
Lighting: Thomas Skelton

THE SONG OF SONGS   *(Duet with company)*

Premiere: August 1947, at the Hatch Memorial Shell,
               Charles River Esplanade, Boston, Massachusetts
Music: *The Song of Songs* by Lucas Foss
Costumes: Pauline Lawrence

SYMPHONY FOR STRINGS   *(Sextet)*

Premiere: August 19, 1955, at the Connecticut College
               American Dance Festival, New London
Music: *Symphony for Strings* by William Schuman
Costumes: Pauline Lawrence

TANGO   *(Duet)*

Premiere: Spring 1931, at the Humphrey-Weidman Studio,
               New York City
Music: Percussion score by José Limón
Costumes: Charles Weidman

TENEBRAE 1914   *(Sextet)*

Premiere: August 13, 1959, at the Connecticut College
               American Dance Festival, New London
Music: *Tenebrae* by John Wilson
Costumes: Pauline Lawrence
Set: Ming Cho Lee
Lighting: Thomas Skelton

THERE IS A TIME
(Ensemble work for 11)

(Variations on a Theme)

Premiere: April 20, 1956, at the Juilliard School of Music, New York City

Music: *Meditation on Ecclesiastes* by Norman Dello Joio

Costumes: Pauline Lawrence

Lighting: Tharon Musser

Daniel Lewis in "A time to be born" from There Is a Time.

THIS STORY IS LEGEND
(Duet)

Premiere: March 1941, Seattle, Washington; choreographed in collaboration with May O'Donnell

Music: *Piano Solo* by Ray Green

Text: *In the American Grain* by William Carlos Williams

Decor and Costumes: Claire Falkenstein

THREE INVENTORIES ON CASEY JONES
(Duet)

Premiere: March 1941, Seattle, Washington; choreographed in collaboration with May O'Donnell

Music: *Three Inventories on Casey Jones* by Ray Green

Costumes: Claire Falkenstein

THREE STUDIES   *(Male solo)*

(These studies were later used in *Danzas Mexicanas*.)

Premiere: October 12, 1935, at the Washington Irving
High School, New York City

Music: Carl Engel

THREE WOMEN   *(Duet)*

(formerly War Lyrics)

Premiere: March 1941, Seattle, Washington; choreographed
in collaboration with May O'Donnell

Music: *Three Women* by Ray Green

Costumes: Claire Falkenstein

TONANTZINTLA   *(Quintet)*

Premiere: March 1951, Palacio de Bellas Artes,
Mexico City

Music: *Four Sonatas* by Fray Antonio Soler

Scenery
and
Costumes: Miguel Covarrubias

THE TRAITOR   *(Ensemble work for 8 men)*

Premiere: August 19, 1954, at the Connecticut College
American Dance Festival, New London

Music: *Symphony for Brasses and Percussion*
by Gunther Schuller

Set: Paul Trautvetter

Costumes: Pauline Lawrence

*José Limón and Louis Falco
in* The Traitor.

TWO ESSAYS FOR LARGE ENSEMBLE   *(Ensemble work for 29)*

(These two pieces are now part of *A Choreographic Offering*.)

Premiere: April 17, 1964, at the Juilliard Concert Hall,
New York City
Music: "Canon A 4" and "Allegro" from *Trio Sonata*
from *A Musical Offering* by Johann Sebastian Bach
Costumes: Pauline Lawrence
Lighting: Sidney Bennett

TWO PRELUDES   *(Male solo)*

Premiere: Spring 1931, at the Humphrey-Weidman Studio,
New York City
Music: Reginald de Koven

Left to right: Charles Hayward, Aaron Osborn, Edward DeSoto, Louis Solino, Clyde Morgan, Jerry Wise and Gary Masters rehearsing The Unsung.

THE UNSUNG   *(Ensemble work for 8 men)*

"This is a paean to the heroic defenders of American Patrimony."

Premiere: May 26, 1970, at the Juilliard Theater as a "work in
progress"
November 5, 1971, at the Walnut Street Theater,
Philadelphia
Costumes: Charles D. Tomlinson

VARIATIONS ON A THEME OF PAGANINI   *(Ensemble work for 10)*

Premiere: February 12, 1965, at the Juilliard Concert Hall, New York City
Music: *Variations on a Theme of Paganini, Op. 35* by Johannes Brahms
Costumes: Charles D. Tomlinson
Lighting: Sidney Bennett

THE VISITATION   *(Trio)*

Premiere: August 23, 1952, at the Connecticut College American Dance Festival, New London
Music: *Piano Pieces, Op. 11, Op. 19, No. 6* by Arnold Schoenberg
Costumes: Pauline Lawrence

WAR LYRICS   *(Duet)*

Premiere: August 1940, at Mills College, Oakland, California; choreographed in collaboration with May O'Donnell
Music: Piano and trumpet score by Esther Williamson
Words: William Archibald
Costumes: José Limón

WESTERN FOLK SUITE   *(Duet)*

Premiere: March 11, 1943, at the Humphrey-Weidman Studio, New York City
Music: *Reel* by Norman Cazden
Ballad of Charlie Rutlage by Charles Ives
Pop Goes the Weasel arranged by Esther Williamson
Costumes: Pauline Lawrence

THE WINGED   *(Ensemble work for 17)*

Premiere: August 20, 1966, at the Connecticut College American Dance Festival, New London
Music: These dances were composed without music and are designed to be performed in silence, with a few exceptions. Incidental music by Hank Johnson
Costumes: Pauline Lawrence
Lighting: Thomas Skelton

Jennifer Muller in The Winged *at the Washington Cathedral.*

OTHER WORKS

1935 A dance-drama produced at Perry-Mansfield Camp, Steamboat Springs, Colorado, Summer 1935

YERMA By Federico García-Lorca
Music by Heitor Villa-Lobos,
with the Sante Fe Opera Company

LAMP UNTO MY FEET, CBS Television series
And David Wept April 11, 1971
Luther June 1972 (not released)

THE WALDSTEIN SONATA, an unfinished work to Beethoven's *Waldstein Sonata,* begun by José Limón just before his death and completed by Daniel Lewis in 1975

Soldier-revues presented while serving in the U.S. Army, 1942–1945

SONG OF THE MEDICS	Fort Dix, New Jersey
DELIVER THE GOODS	Camp Lee, Virginia
We Speak for Ourselves in **FUN FOR THE BIRDS**	Camp Lee, Virginia
CHRISTMAS PAGEANT	Camp Lee, Virginia

CHRONOLOGICAL LISTING BY DATE OF PREMIERE

1930   BACCHANALE
ÉTUDE IN D FLAT MAJOR

1931   PETITE SUITE
TANGO
TWO PRELUDES

1932   BACH SUITE

1933   CANCIÓN Y DANZA
DANZA (Prokofiev)
PIÈCES FROIDES

1935   THREE STUDIES
NOSTALGIC FRAGMENTS
PRELUDE

1936   SATIRIC LAMENT
HYMN

1937   DANZA DE LA MUERTE

1939   DANZAS MEXICANAS

1940   WAR LYRICS

1941   CURTAIN RAISER
THIS STORY IS LEGEND
THREE INVENTORIES ON CASEY JONES
THREE WOMEN (formerly WAR LYRICS)

1942   CHACONNE

1943   WESTERN FOLK SUITE

1945   CONCERTO GROSSO
EDEN TREE
DANZA (Arcadio)

1946	MASQUERADE
1947	LA MALINCHE THE SONG OF SONGS
1949	THE MOOR'S PAVANE
1950	THE EXILES CONCERT
1951	LOS CUATROS SOLES DIALOGUES ANTIGONA TONANTZINTLA THE QUEEN'S EPICEDIUM REDES
1952	THE VISITATION EL GRITO (formerly REDES)
1953	DON JUAN FANTASIA
1954	ODE TO THE DANCE THE TRAITOR
1955	SCHERZO (Barracuda, Lincoln, Venable) SCHERZO (Johnson) SYMPHONY FOR STRINGS
1956	THERE IS A TIME (Variations on a Theme) KING'S HEART THE EMPEROR JONES
1957	BLUE ROSES
1958	MISSA BREVIS SERENATA DANCES
1959	TENEBRAE 1914 THE APOSTATE
1960	BARREN SCEPTRE

1961	PERFORMANCE THE MOIRAI SONATA FOR TWO CELLOS
1962	I, ODYSSEUS
1963	THE DEMON
1964	TWO ESSAYS FOR LARGE ENSEMBLE A CHOREOGRAPHIC OFFERING
1965	VARIATIONS ON A THEME OF PAGANINI MY SON, MY ENEMY
1966	THE WINGED
1967	MAC ABER'S DANCE PSALM
1968	COMEDY LEGEND
1969	LA PIÑATA
1970	THE UNSUNG (as a work in progress)
1971	REVEL THE UNSUNG DANCES FOR ISADORA
1972	ORFEO CARLOTA

SOURCES

Chronologies of works by José Limón, compiled by Juliette Waung and Sheldon Schwartz. From the files of the Dance Division of the Juilliard School, Lincoln Center, New York City, Martha Hill, Director.

The New York Public Library and Museum of Performing Arts, Lincoln Center, New York City.

Personal knowledge of the works of José Limón.

Labanotation

Labanotation is a system of recording the dance movements by indicating, through the use of symbols, what each part of the body does and where it moves. Phrasing, counts and tempo are included to give a more complete picture of how a movement is executed, not just physically but temporally as well. For the choreographer, Labanotation provides a way of documenting each movement in a dance so that it can be reconstructed. The notation may be augmented by photos, films, written descriptions and commentary by the choreographer and original cast.

In this book, the exercises have been set down as clearly and accurately as possible in words and drawings. The Labanotation is provided for those who know how to read and use it.

The following Labanotation of the exercises is by Mary Corey, checked by Ilene Fox, autographed by Lynne Allard and certified by the Dance Notation Bureau.

GLOSSARY

1. It is assumed that persons using the Labanotation in this book will first have read the text. Therefore, imagery word-notes have not been included with the notation.

2. *Successional arms:* below left is the completely notated version of successional arms (see page 40). The abbreviated version, on the right, is the version that will appear in the Exercises.

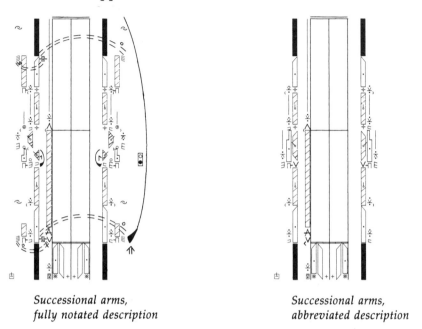

Successional arms,
fully notated description

Successional arms,
abbreviated description

3. The arms' ◇ and ○ have not been written for exercises in which the body circles (advanced version of pliés, swings in second and in rebound in threes). The reader should move the arms in a relaxed, unemphasized manner as shown in the following examples:

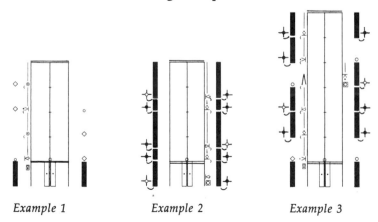

Example 1   *Example 2*   *Example 3*

4. 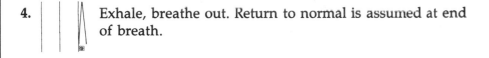 Exhale, breathe out. Return to normal is assumed at end of breath.

5. The black diamond (◆) placed within a direction symbol indicates undeviating aim with direction judged from the *new* front.

6.) Initiation bow. The symbol inside the bow shows which body part initiates the movement. For example:) means initiate with the right shoulder.

7. 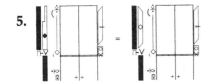 Design drawing. The specified body part traces the design indicated in the path sign. The starting point for the design is shown by a dot. The design is drawn on the surface specified within the path sign (⊞ , the place low surface). For further information, consult the 1979 I.C.K.L. proceedings.

8. /\ Disappear, cease to be in effect.

9. = Modern dance turnout.

10. Presigns for the legs have been omitted. For example:

11. The placement of a tick on a minor movement pin indicates distal center analysis. The direction and level of the deviation are judged from the extremity. For further information, consult the 1979 I.C.K.L. proceedings.

12. ⌠ Passive weight.

13. An ad-lib sign within a direction symbol refers to level only.

SUCCESSIONAL BODY MOVEMENT

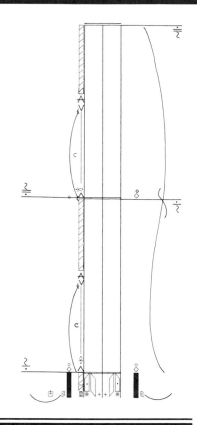

ONE: SPINAL SUCCESSION

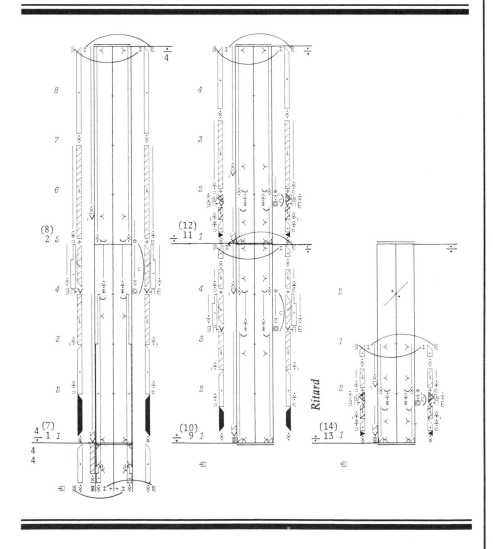

TWO: BOUNCES

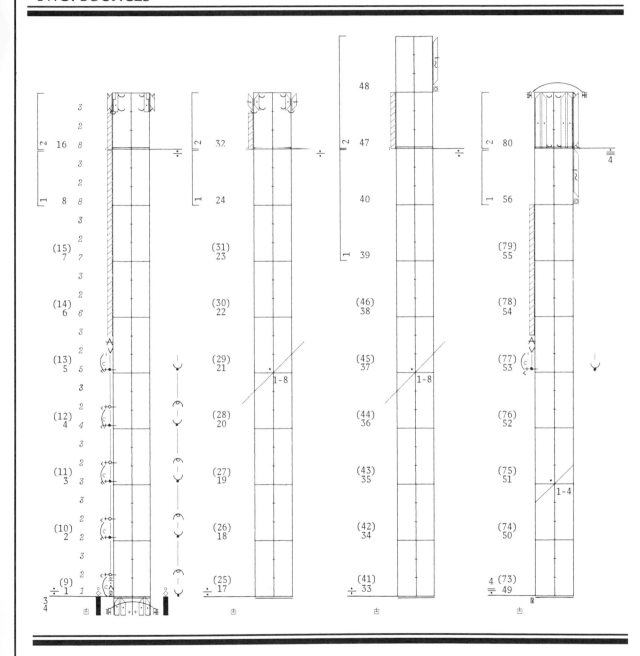

TWO: BOUNCES (*continued*)

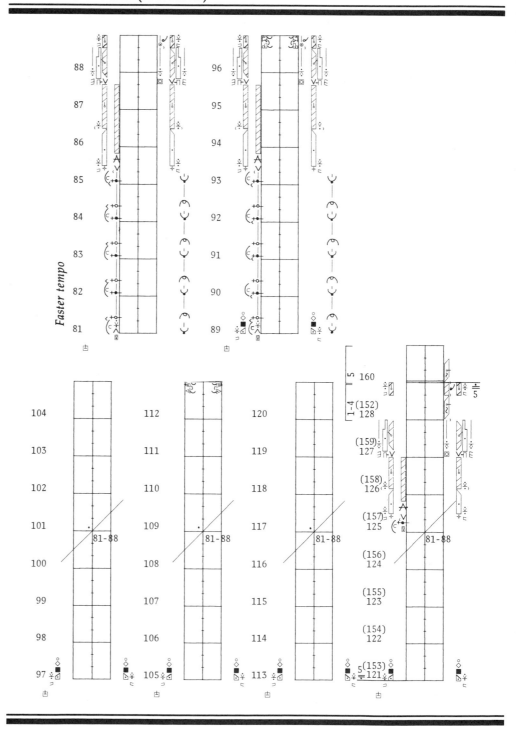

Faster tempo

THREE: BOUNCES WITH TWIST

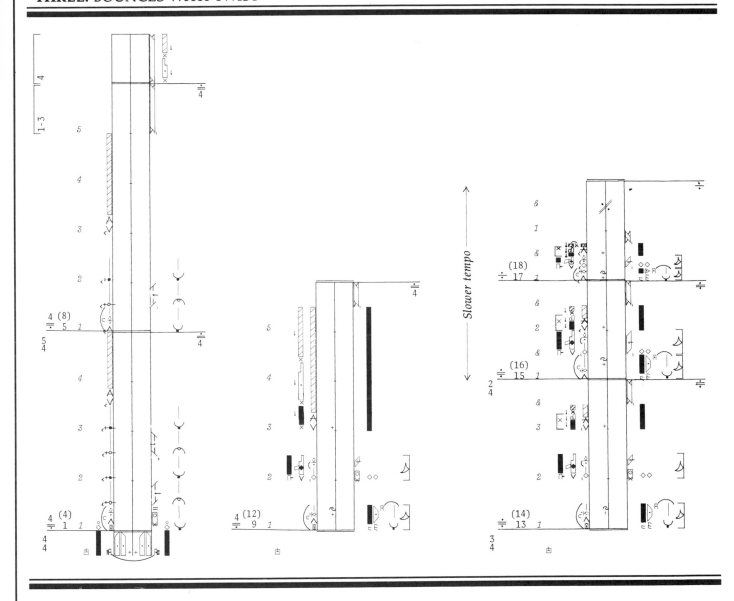

FOUR: STANDING BOUNCES

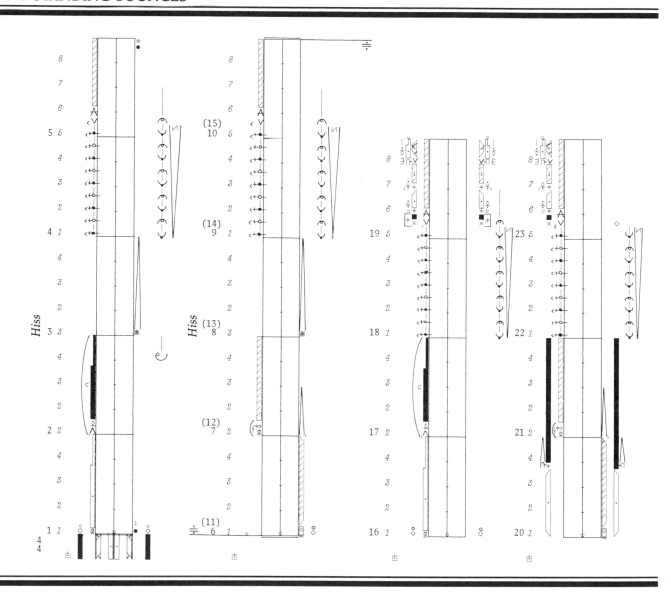

FIVE: TENDU SERIES

Half turn optional

17-20

49-52

SIX: PLIE SERIES

Preparation

6   6   6

5   5   5

4   4   4

3   3   3

2   2   2

1   1 *1*   (3) 2 *1*

6
4

6   6   6

5   5   5

4   4   4

3   3   3

2   2   2

4 *1*   (6) 5 *1*   4 (10) 7 *1*

Intermediate version   *Advanced version*

SEVEN: SWINGS IN SECOND

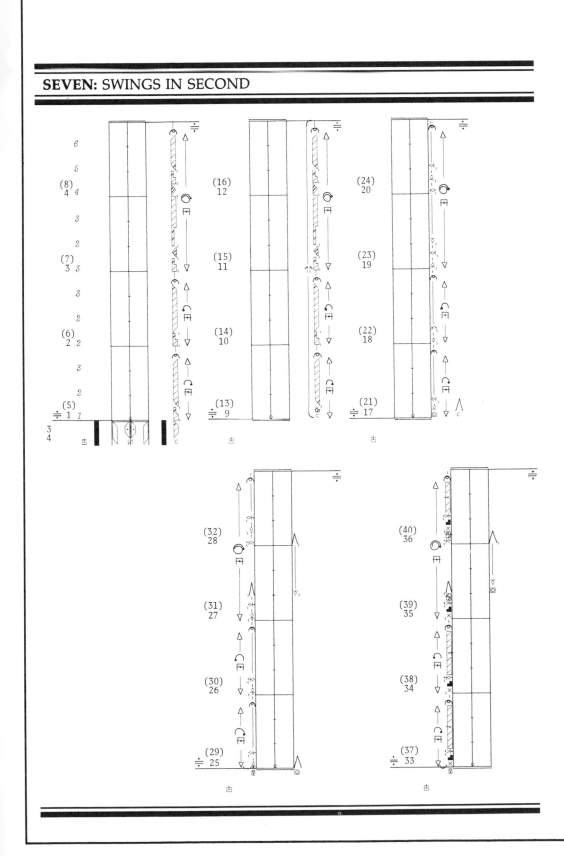

EIGHT: REBOUNDS IN THREES

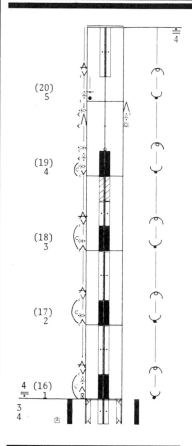

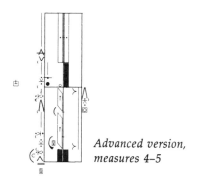

Advanced version, measures 4–5

NINE: SLOW TWOS, FAST THREES

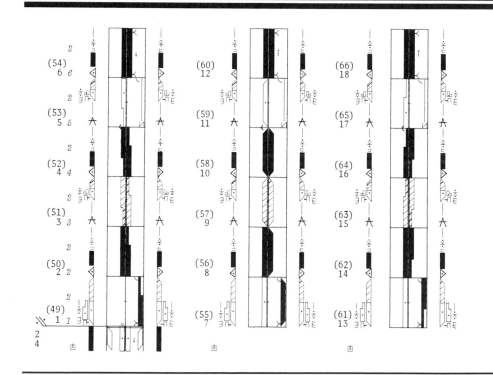

NINE: SLOW TWOS, FAST THREES (*continued*)

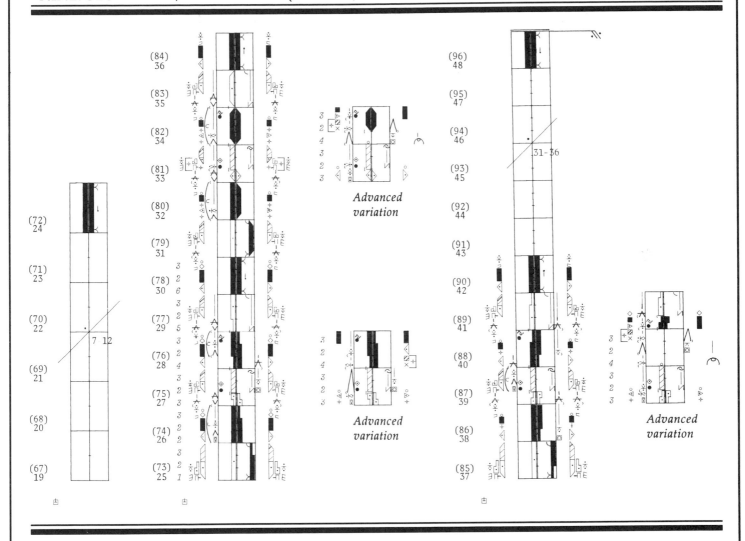

Advanced variation

Advanced variation

Advanced variation

TEN: FOOT ISOLATIONS

ELEVEN: PASSÉ SERIES

Plain turns

Slower tempo

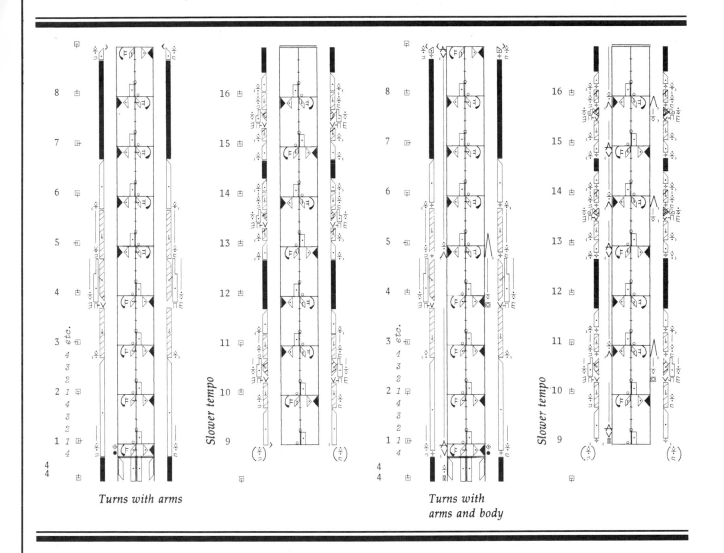

Turns with arms

Slower tempo

Turns with
arms and body

Slower tempo

TWELVE: DEVELOPPÉ SERIES

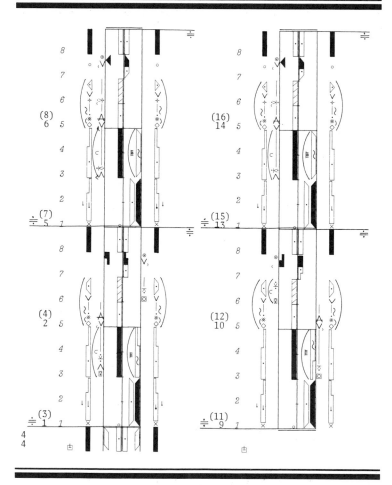

THIRTEEN: LUNGE SERIES

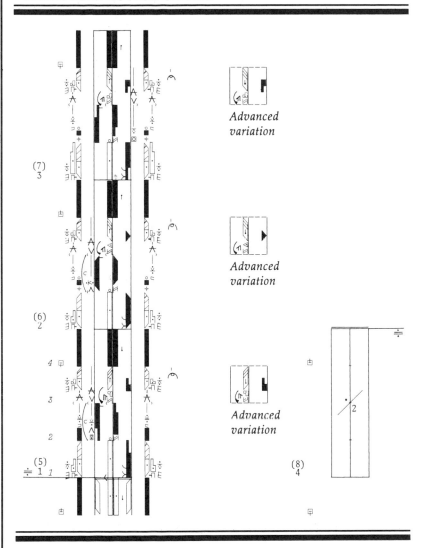

Advanced variation

Advanced variation

Advanced variation

FOURTEEN: SPIRAL TURNS

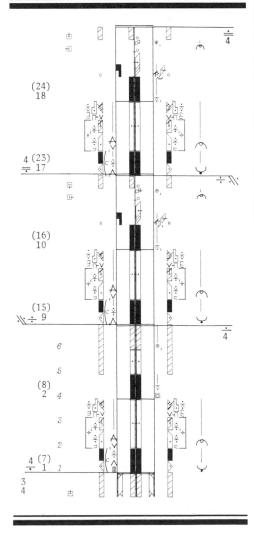

FIFTEEN: 12-COUNT PHRASE

Preparation 1 _Preparation 2_ _Intermediate_ _Advanced_

SIXTEEN: DROPS IN THREES

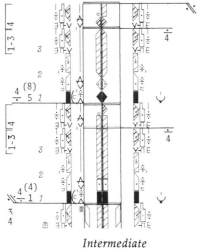

*Intermediate
version*

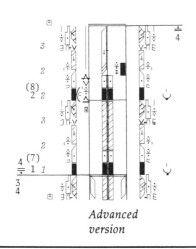

*Advanced
version*

SEVENTEEN: JUMPS

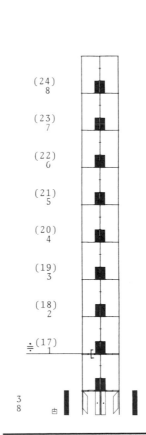

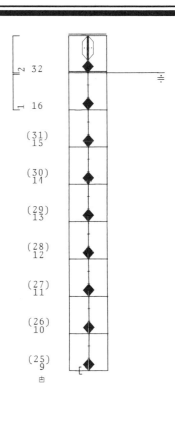

EIGHTEEN: THE BODY AS AN ORCHESTRA

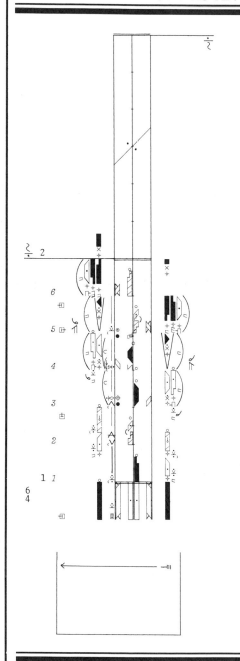

NINETEEN: HOP SERIES

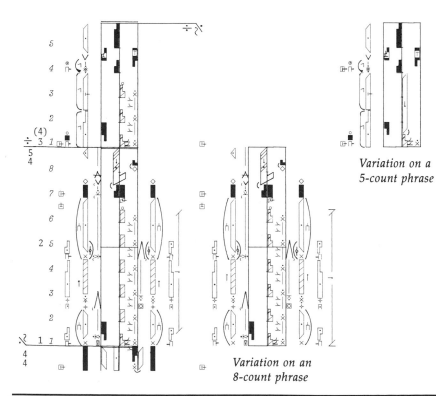

*Variation on a
5-count phrase*

*Variation on an
8-count phrase*

TWENTY: PIQUÉ SERIES

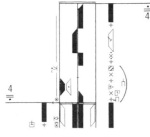

*Advanced
version*

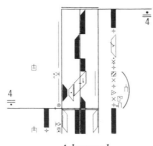

*Advanced
variation 2*

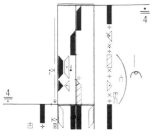

*Intermediate
version*

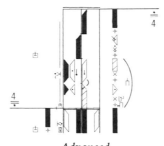

*Advanced
variation 1*

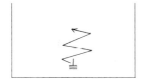

FROM *MISSA BREVIS*

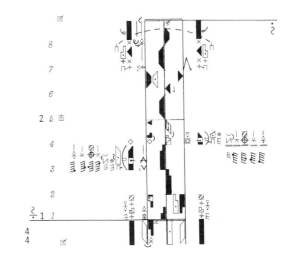

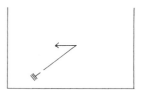

Notes

1. Capezio Dance Award, 11 March 1964.
2. Limón, "The Modern Dance as an Unpopular Art."
3. Chapin, "Dance: Limón's Means of Survival."
4. McDonagh, *Martha Graham*, 64.
5. Ibid., 65.
6. Humphrey, *Doris Humphrey*, 85.
7. McDonagh, *Martha Graham*, 59.
8. Martin, "The Dancer as an Artist."
9. Limón, from his unpublished autobiography.
10. Martin, "The Dancer as an Artist."
11. Limón, "Dancers Are Musicians Are Dancers," from a convocation address given at the Juilliard School, 5 October 1966.
12. Beiswanger, "Doris Humphrey and Company, with José Limón." [Note: author has right and left reversed in his description. It should be downstage right and upstage left.]
13. Barnes, "Dance: The Subtle Poetry of 'Othello.'"
14. Martin, "Limón Work Given at Dance Festival."
15. Jowitt, "Allies of the Ground; Eye on the Sky."
16. Martin, "The Dance: Limón."
17. _____, "The Dancer as an Artist."
18. Chapin, "Dance: Limón's Means of Survival."
19. _____, "José Limón and Dancers at Philharmonic Hall."
20. Jowitt, "Dance."
21. Siegel, "Limón Performs 4 New Works."
22. Ibid.
23. Lewis, "Remembering José Limón."
24. Limón, "Young Dancers State Their Views."
25. Martin, "The Dancer as an Artist."
26. Wessels, "Dance."

Bibliography

BOOKS

Cohen, Selma Jeanne, ed. *The Modern Dance: Seven Statements of Belief.* Middletown, Conn.: Wesleyan University Press, 1965.

Humphrey, Doris. *Doris Humphrey: An Artist First.* Edited by Selma Jeanne Cohen. Middletown, Conn.: Wesleyan University Press, 1972.

Jowitt, Deborah. *Dance Beat.* New York: Marcel Dekker, 1977.

McDonagh, Don. *Martha Graham.* New York: Praeger, 1973.
_____. *The Rise and Fall and Rise of Modern Dance.* New York: New American Library, 1971.

Siegel, Marcia B. *The Shapes of Change.* Boston: Houghton Mifflin, 1979.

Terry, Walter. *The Dance in America.* New York: Harper & Row, 1971.

ARTICLES AND REVIEWS

Barnes, Clive. "As a Dancer, an Eagle." *New York Times,* 4 December 1972.
_____. "Dance: The Subtle Poetry of 'Othello.'" *New York Times,* January 1972.

Beiswanger, George W. "Doris Humphrey and Company, with José Limón." *Dance Observer* 10 (February 1943).

Chapin, Louis. "Dance: Limón's Means of Survival." *Christian Science Monitor,* 10 February 1966.
_____. "José Limón and Dancers at Philharmonic Hall." *Christian Science Monitor,* 8 January 1963.

Jowitt, Deborah. "Allies of the Ground; Eye on the Sky." *Village Voice,* 15 November 1973.
_____. "Dance." *Village Voice,* 18 November 1971.

Lewis, Jean Battey. "Remembering José Limón." *Washington Post,* 17 December 1972.

Limón, José. "Composing a Dance." *The Juillard Review* 2 (Winter 1955): 18.

———. "The Modern Dance as an Unpopular Art." *The Juillard Review Annual* (1964–65): 31.

———. "On Constancy." Speech given at the opening of the twentieth Connecticut College American Dance Festival, 1967.

———. "On Dance." *Seven Arts*, 1953 (n.d.).

———. "On Magic." Speech given at the Connecticut College American Dance Festival, 8 July 1968.

———. "Young Dancers State Their Views." *Dance Observer*, 1946.

Martin, John. "The Dance: Limón." *New York Times*, 10 April 1949.

———. "The Dancer as an Artist." *New York Times Magazine*, 12 April 1953.

———. "Limón Work Given at Dance Festival." *New York Times*, 21 August 1949.

Siegel, Marcia B. "Limón Performs 4 New Works." *Boston Globe*, 22 October 1972.

Wessels, Frances. "Dance." *Richmond Times-Dispatch*, 20 February 1965.

OTHER

Unpublished writings of José Limón: letters and other materials from the José Limón Papers and the Pauline Lawrence Limón Papers at the Dance Collection of the New York Public Library for the Performing Arts at Lincoln Center, from the files of the Juilliard School, and from the personal files of Daniel Lewis.